HOME-BASED BUSINESS SERIES

how to start a home-based

Computer Repair Business

Ryan Arter

Guilford, Connecticut

Dedicated to my father, Gary A. Arter,
who was unable to see the completion of this book . . .
but without whom it would have never been accomplished.

To buy books in quantity for corporate use
or incentives, call **(800) 962-0973**
or e-mail **premiums@GlobePequot.com**.

Interior spot art licensed by Shutterstock.com.

Editorial Director: Cynthia Hughes Cullen
Editor: Tracee Williams
Project Editor: Lauren Brancato
Text Design: Sheryl P. Kober
Layout: Nancy Freeborn

ISBN 978-0-7627-8658-9
ISSN 2327-9435

Printed in the United States of America
10 9 8 7 6 5 4 3 2 1

Contents

Acknowledgments

I would like to express my greatest gratitude to the people who have helped and supported me throughout the writing of this book. I am grateful to my wife, Dandra, for her continuous support, from initial advice in the early stages to consistent encouragement to this day.

Writing a book is an interesting adventure, and I'm sure from the outside world it seemed that I fell into a black hole as my keyboard took its punishment. Nothing good comes easy, and I have reached a new level of self-worth, tenacity, and patience. This project has made me a better person in the world in which we all coexist.

I wish to thank my parents for their undivided support and interest. They inspired me and encouraged me to go my own way, and without them I would not feel success at any level. Last but not least, I want to thank my children, Jordyn, Tayler, and Casey, who give me purpose and happy memories each day . . .

Introduction

So you're interested in starting your own computer repair business? Every business starts with an idea, then that idea is explored. You have the makings of being an entrepreneur.

When you look at small business in America, there is an overwhelming number of small businesses, specifically businesses that have between one and four employees. One reason for this is because the US offers opportunity, prosperity, and the freedom for entrepreneurs to make their ideas become a reality.

The word "entrepreneur" was first defined as a person who pays a certain price for a product to resell at a different price. I'm a believer that entrepreneurs are innovators who shatter the status quo and take advantage of good ideas to invent new products and services that are valuable, and therefore profitable, to consumers.

There are several reasons why you might want to start your own business. It's a very personal thing. For me, I had been laid off in the past, and I found my work at other businesses nerve-wracking. On a daily basis, my coworkers were being laid off, I could see misuse of funds, and there was constant talk about "downsizing"—until my corporate managers started to notice the drop in morale, so it became "right-sizing." In any case, workers feared for their jobs and working in a state of fear was a stress I didn't want.

Having spent a portion of my adult life in corporate positions, I knew I could go job-hunting. But I wasn't looking for another "secure" position to be shot out from under me, whether through downsizing, restructuring, or other reorganization. With a wife and three children to clothe and feed, I was no longer willing to trust my future to this game of corporate roulette.

I then reentered the small-business arena. No more suit and tie, a more relaxed atmosphere, and no more corporate meetings. I found myself happier, more productive, and motivated. However, I was still at the mercy of my employers in terms of growth potential and money-making capability. Then came the talks of "layoff" again and I realized that I needed to be in control of my own destiny. I wanted to own my own business. It was time to go into business for myself.

From the first day of starting my business, I accepted the fact that it might not work. However, I always said that if I was going to go out of business (or not have a job), then it was going to be on my terms. This holds true today. I had a firm belief in myself, my ideas, and my work ethic. I figured that the time was right for me to stop relying on another business for employment and to rely on myself. After ten years, I have never looked back.

Across the country and around the world, millions of people are abandoning their dependence on big businesses and seeking independence through their own enterprises. Every month, about one million Americans go through some type of job loss or change, and more small businesses are being created. The movement is astounding.

In a recent report titled "Work, Entrepreneurship and Opportunity in 21st Century America," the US Chamber of Commerce said, "Millions of Americans are embracing entrepreneurship by running their own small businesses, through independent contracting or direct selling." The report also cited a recent Gallup poll finding that 61 percent of Americans now say they prefer to be their own bosses.

There are many benefits of entrepreneurship:

- Freedom. I love the benefits of working for myself, specifically the freedom. Not just the thought of being able to come and go as I please—in fact, more and more I think my businesses tie me up rather than free my time. I'm talking about the freedom to make your own decisions. The freedom to try something new. The freedom to reap the rewards of your own hard work rather than have someone else reaping them for you. And you do get to choose when to work, what you're going to do on a daily basis, and what comes next for yourself.

- Job Security. Not long ago, starting your own business was considered risky and foolish. "Get a job with a large firm" was what I heard for many years. With more and more "large firms" cutting pensions and retirement plans, my worries were piqued. Since there are a lot of "logical" decisions to make in running your own business, I felt that I could easily and simply attack it from a logical perspective. Logic works. You can create your own destiny and your own job security by running an honest, innovative business that also doubles as your retirement plan as it grows. Count on yourself.

■ Flexibility. With the invention of the computer and the Internet, the possibility of starting your own business is easier than you think. From the comfort of your own home, you can market yourself with a website and online advertising and operate a truly competitive business without the expense of a commercial location. From your computer, you can reach local, nationwide, and worldwide customers via geo-targeting. The flexibility that is afforded by today's technology is amazing, and being flexible is one of the keys to success.

■ Making More Money. The opportunity to make more money by building your own empire makes sense. In a corporate job, you may have a nice salary and even a bonus plan, but more often than not, you don't have the ability to make more when you work harder. This ability is the basis of small business. If you're ready to get to work, you have an open-ended option to make your "American Dream" become a reality.

When you're in business for yourself, you're writing your own script, your own reality. You write your own history as you're creating your own success story—you then write your own paycheck. When you're in business for yourself you have the opportunity to believe in what you're doing and to be passionate about your business.

■ Pride. Undoubtedly, the vision of your new business has many aspects. Maybe you can imagine what the name will be. Maybe you can image yourself in front of your customers. It's possible you're looking forward to opening your first retail location. Maybe quite simply, just being able to say "I own a business" to your peers, family members, and new acquaintances sounds appealing to you. It is.

Owning a successful business does bring pride. Being proud of your accomplishments is not a bad thing—in fact, pride is an emotion that many entrepreneurs describe having as they continue their careers within their own business. Pride results from hard work, and hard work is regarded as an admirable trait. It's good to be proud of your business—you built it and it has your characteristics, blood, sweat, and tears all wrapped up into it. You'll find that pride is closely linked to your passion, motivation, and success.

Is It Time for You to Take the Leap of Faith?

"Leaving the rat race is not as daunting as it may seem," says author Dan Clements in his guide to work/life balance, *Escape 101*. "You'll look back in later years and marvel at how easy it was and how much you gained for so little cost."

So what does it take? First, let's look at what it doesn't take. You don't need an MBA or high-powered business background, and you don't need to be rich or to take a second mortgage on your home. Some of the most successful business owners in the world are not college educated, and that's admirable. You will find that there are lessons in business ownership that you can't read in a college textbook or learn from a professor in a classroom.

There are some self-owned business opportunities that require specialized expertise, such as consulting, or others that can take significant capital investment and possible training, such as real estate investing and franchises, but some can be started on a limited budget and prove quite lucrative, including direct selling and online opportunities. Many of the greatest entrepreneurs of our time began with no advanced degrees and hardly any start-up capital. They merely had the belief in themselves to make the magic happen.

On your quest to make a life for yourself as a small-business owner providing computer repair, the answers are all out there for you. This is a growth industry and it's obvious that computers are not a trendy "flash in the pan" type of product. Our lives are surrounded by computers—for example, I'm writing this book on one now. The need for more computer repair businesses in the field is great, and while there is some competition the demand greatly outweighs supply. It may be time to write your own destiny.

But make no mistake about it, what you save in up-front cash you will make up for in sweat equity and passion. The major investment in most self-owned businesses is investment of one's self in the form of time, focus, and persistence. You don't need to be a genius at negotiation or a genius at numbers, and you can take a simple, logical approach. The bottom line is that you will need a burning desire and determination fueled by a strong dose of passion!

01 So You Want to Start a Home-Based Computer Repair Business

You've got to have an entrepreneur's spirit if you want to go into business for yourself. Clearly, you have a feeling about the electronics industry. Let's face it. It's cool, cutting edge, and the newest handheld electronics are astounding. Just take a look at today's smartphones: They are able to play movies, connect to car navigation systems, keep your calendar, play music, and perform a plethora of other functions all while fitting in the palm of your hand.

I noticed a real need for an electronics repair company just by watching my friends. They would carelessly toss around their phones and computers and then complain about them as they stopped working or started to have intermittent problems. Frankly I saw an opportunity. I figured that there were so many devices out in the world that all I needed to do was offer a legitimate service, run a little advertising, charge fair prices, and the orders would start coming in. I was right.

I'm not going to sugar-coat this for you. Starting a business is not an easy task. In fact there are many great ideas out there, like great opportunities that sit stagnant because taking the leap into the self-employment world is scary and downright impossible for some people. Again, it's not easy, but people are doing it every day. There are many reasons why people would dive into their own business. It gives you a passion for your work, you will walk through life with pride, and the rewards (financial and otherwise) can be great.

If you know people who own a business, you will find that they are tough and worldly. This comes from the real battles that business owners wage on a daily basis. I personally admire other business owners, and as you read this you're taking the first step to owning your own business. I admire you too.

Good luck on your endeavor and remember that it can be done. Hard work pays off, and you can trust in yourself.

Your Love of Electronics

Were you the kid who took apart his father's home stereo and was able to put it back together again? Or maybe it never worked again but you were just drawn to the electronics and the engineering involved? I love electronics and as a youngster I was always drawn to capacitors, diodes, and electricity in general.

Moving into my adult life the thought of being around cutting-edge devices was always very exciting and being the first to own these kinds of devices was a goal of mine. I mean who doesn't want the next newest and greatest thing? Well, money usually stood in my way of buying new, expensive electronics every month as they came out so I started a computer repair business that catered to computer owners as well as anyone with a smartphone, MP3 player, or tablet. The logic was that most gadgets today have a definite useful life, and while having the newest and greatest device is fun and intriguing, it isn't financially feasible for everyone. Instead, I found that customers needed a viable solution to keep their not-yet-outdated devices operating correctly. My idea of starting a business to keep expensive gadgets in operation while saving customers money was going to be the basis of a successful business. I most certainly also have plans to expand into other areas of service as well, as new technology emerges.

Technology has developed so drastically over the last twenty years that it's amazing to think about how far we have come in such a short amount of time. In 1992 (that's over twenty years ago), the first portable computer—better known now as a laptop—was invented, and it was called the "freedom machine." The next year, the World Wide Web had only 130 accessible sites.

In 1994, the first blog was created. Over the next ten or so years, innumerable companies such as hotels and airfare providers began advertising online. Google was first launched in 1998, with Wikipedia following soon after in 2000. The first iPod was released in 2001. The first Wi-Fi hotspot was not created until 2003.

In the past ten years, so much new technology has been created that naming all the innovations could fill a whole book. Flat-screen TVs, digital cameras, smartphones, Facebook, DVDs, online gaming, hybrid cars, the Wii (and many other gaming platforms), and eBay—to name just a few.

If these items don't interest you then maybe a computer repair business is not in your future. However, with seemingly endless new technology appearing the world over on a consistent basis, it's difficult for some of us not to get excited. The industry needs more computer repair centers and yours might be the next success!

Computer Repair Is a Service Business

There's no question that a service business can be made or broken simply by bad customer experiences. If doesn't matter if your business is the low-price leader, if your business has the best website, or if you hit a home run and land a large customer. If your service is bad, you won't stay in business.

The word "service" originates from the Latin word *servitium,* which means "condition of a slave." While you might think that you're a slave to your customers, you are not. But you are a slave to your business and serving your customers should be the number-one priority in your plan.

The service business is around to cater to consumers in need who are looking for ways to make life easier on themselves, and some services are more needed than others.

Unfortunately the service industry can get a bad rap at times. Have you ever visited a car mechanic and questioned whether or not you really needed that extra thingamajig that he quoted when you simply brought your car in for an oil change?

At times your customers might immediately put you behind a shroud of mistrust even before you make a sale. It'll be your job to convince them otherwise.

The computer repair industry is a multibillion-dollar industry and your piece of the pie is just waiting for you in the market. Your customers will expect the expert (you) to deliver timely, effective, and budget-friendly services based on your use of sales techniques. This sounds easy enough, but what I can really boil it down to is:

Do what you say you'll do.

Trust me, at the end of the day your customers won't care about how nicely you dressed, how impressive your brochures were, or even how great a price you gave them if you botch the service aspect of your service-based business. You'll quickly be looking for a job in the open market with a failed business on your résumé. Instead, go into each sale and build a relationship with each customer and remember to do what you say you'll do. This wins customers, sparks word-of-mouth advertising, and gives you the competitive advantage.

Customer service is the name of the game. There are so many businesses that follow a philosophy of "that's good enough," but when you're trying to make a mark in this industry, it's never good enough. Does that mean you have to go far above and beyond your customer's expectations? No, but that will help. Truly, excellence is what differentiates a successful, quality business from an ordinary one. Treat each customer as a person; as the salesperson for your business, you'll want to give him or her your undivided attention. Really listen to customers and understand their needs and the potential issues that may arise. You are in the service business, so be the consummate professional and provide excellent solutions. Never react in a negative way to any situation, if possible. Remember that to the customer, you're the "business," making money from them, so they may feel the "right" to become angry, demanding, or even insulting. It's your job to stay cool, and a good business owner can turn these situations around into positive outcomes.

Don't let your customers find a competitor. If you provide good customer service, they will remember you for that, tell their friends, and your business will grow.

The Life of an Owner/Operator

I can clearly remember my very first day being self-employed. I was a nervous wreck, sitting at my kitchen table wondering, "What's next?" My first hurdle was just being overwhelmed with where to start, what to do first, and when I was going to get paid. These concerns had to be put out of my mind, and personally I'm the kind of guy who needs to focus on what can be done in a logical manner. It was a discipline that has kept me employed in the past, so I applied it to my new business.

There's no question that finances will quickly become an issue in your new venture. This topic is never easy, and you constantly hear "it takes money to make money." Well, this is true in many ways, but a good business plan and a lot of hard work are what really make money, and you may not need as many "Benjamins" as you think to get started.

Here's a quick table that will give you a rough idea of what your monthly spending will be when starting up your business. Take a few minutes to think about all of your life expenses and trim the unnecessary items for now. Unless you are made of money, the luxuries should be put on hold and your free cash should be used on your business—your future. Let's take a look at your monthly expenses.

Being successful takes a lot of hard work, but for me in the beginning it was mostly worrying. There's no denying one thing—being self-employed means that you're always working in some form or fashion whether it be in bed, in the shower, or at your desk. If you have a brain that can run twenty-four hours a day, it will. Until you see some success, you'll need to train yourself to not panic and to attack the tasks that are doable.

It's a great idea to get your expenses in line so you know what you can afford and when. This simple spreadsheet gives an idea of what your expenses may be. Just add or subtract your personal expenses and your business expenses as required. This example shows beginning cash, aka your "start-up cash," as $10,000, removes your monthly bills and start-up purchases, then reveals your remaining income. Notice that your income is $0 in this example. You'd change this to your actual income after you take your first paycheck!

1st Month Expenses

EXPENSE	AMOUNT DUE	DUE DATE	STATUS
Personal			
Electric Bill	$145.00	13th	Paid
Water Bill	$71.00	15th	Open
Insurances	$139.00	4th	Paid
Mortgage	$1,215.00	1st	Paid
Auto Loan	$320.00	28th	Open
Business			
Internet Service	$62.00	12th	Open
Telephone Service	$88.00	19th	Open
Website	$99.00	13th	Paid
Beginning Inventory	$1,830.00	N/A	Open
New Computer	$829.00	N/A	Paid
Work Bench	$520.00	N/A	Paid
Beginning Cash	$10,000.00		
Income	$0.00		
Monthly Expenses	$5,318.00		
Remaining Income	$4,682.00		

What you'll end up with is a fulfilling life. Just think about the times that you'll be able to proudly state that you're self-employed. It's one of my greatest rewards and when I describe it to others, it's usually sounds something like:

"I love being self-employed. I've been laid off before, dealt with unfair managers, even hated my boss in the past. At least I know that if I make it, it'll be because of me and if I fail, it'll be because of me. The one thing that I can truly count on is myself. I don't want to leave my fate in someone else's hands."

I can count on myself. That's the first and most important part about being an owner/operator. You have to believe it and you have to live by it. Without you, your business will never get off the ground. Count on yourself and you'll find successes in all aspects of your life, which is especially true for your new business.

The bottom line is that being a business owner is like a roller-coaster ride. The "highs" are high and the "lows" are low. There's a price for admission and you might not like the ride, but my guess is that you might be nervous as you stand in line, but once you step off you'll be smiling and happy.

Every morning when you begin work at your business, you'll be waiting in the same line and climbing onto this roller coaster knowing that you'll experience exhilaration, speed, and stomach-cramping drops. Now is the time to decide whether you're the adrenaline-junkie roller-coaster fanatic or the slow-paced, carousel-riding kind of person.

Do You Have What It Takes to Be a Repair Technician?

Before becoming self-employed you should analyze yourself and attempt to create a balance between your business and personal life. Remember that being self-employed means that you'll never truly stop working, but you will want to separate and continue to nurture your personal relationships and responsibilities that make you you.

As you look at yourself you're going to want to make sure that this service industry is right for you. A computer repair technician needs to be mechanically inclined with good eyesight. Additionally, there are days where the repair work is repetitive and monotonous and at times can be downright boring. There are also days when it will seem that no matter what you do, you won't be able to fix a device, while you have your customer breathing down your neck. In an instant your mood and business can change, and you're going to want to adapt and embrace those changes.

Expect these things to happen, and expect that you're not going to "know it all" as you receive your first customer. What you'll do is simply rely on your training—whether you're self-taught, learned your computer repair skills on the job, or formally trained in a classroom.

The mind of the repair technician needs to be logical and methodical. Diagnosing a customer's computer problem can be time-consuming and frustrating. Not to worry. After a few hundred repairs you'll know your service line in and out and it will be second nature to you. It's the learning process that will take its toll mentally and physically. However, it's also what makes you an expert and a trustworthy member of the service industry.

I have personally found that technical work is extremely rewarding and fulfilling. There's no better feeling than doing the job right and hearing a customer say "thank you" for delivering your service as promised. This should appeal to you as a technician because as you grow your business you will hear this gratitude more and more. You should look forward to building the customer testimonial page on your website!

Training & Certification

There are a few schools of thought here, speaking of "schools" and training. From the outsider's perspective, diving into a technical job of repairing computers can seem overwhelming and out of reach. What do you do when you want to know more about a field and become an expert? Education comes to mind, in one form or another.

Becoming proficient at almost any job needs patience and time. As a new business owner, you might not have the luxury of having either, but you're a different breed and can handle the challenges that will come at you.

It's true that you'll never regret getting that college education because once you have it, it's yours. That diploma is part of your life and part of your marketability. In your business you need marketing, and your education will come in handy, even if your degree is in an unrelated field.

There are specialized fields of education that can also become part of your marketing program. Trade schools, individualized training programs, and certifications are also quick and effective ways to learn. Community colleges and vocational schools also offer classes from beginning to advanced curriculums that can assist you in your endeavors.

Compile all of that education and top it off with a dose of common sense and you'll be ready for the life you've been craving, the life of a business owner in a market that seems to be never-ending.

Your College Education

Students who attend college do so for very different reasons. Some know exactly what they want to do in life for a career, go to college for the appropriate education, and do it. Some think they know what they want to do, and go to college only to end up changing their minds. Others will go to college not having a clue as to what they want out of life, find a major, and get a diploma.

Then there are students like me, who started college but never finished. I had bigger plans in life (or maybe I just couldn't hack it). Some people are built for the classroom and others are not.

There's no trick here. College is for some people. It can give you direction, a purpose, and even a job when you need it. However, there is no requirement to have a college education when you own a business. Once you're your own boss, you'll never be interviewed again (you'll do the interviewing), and you can rest on the success of your business as you grow. Some of the most successful people in our industry do not have college educations (for example, Steve Jobs at Apple, Inc. and Bill Gates at Microsoft, who dropped out of school in 1975 as a sophomore).

The point is that if you have your degree, it will not hurt you; however, if you don't, there's no rush to finish before you start your business. It's something you can save for when you retire!

Technical School

A technical school, also known as a vocational college or trade school, is an educational institution that prepares students for a career in a specific field. There are many great electronic technical schools across the country and students are taught skills for their career choices directly.

A technical school is a great way to learn the "technician" tools of the trade. Most schools offer programs that are two years or less, and some programs are designed so that a student can transfer credits to a four-year college if needed.

The courses offered at technical schools vary, but many provide training in electronics and information technology that can be of great value and marketability. They will teach you actual skills in addition to theory. Most technical school programs maintain a workplace environment as opposed to a traditional classroom environment, where attendance is obligatory and professional conduct is maintained. The instructors at technical schools are typically trained professionals in the field with experience in a related field.

Many of these schools will provide a certificate upon completion, and tuition costs are typically less than those at most state colleges or universities. Depending on the job skill to be studied, traits that are important for students pursuing technical school training include good manual dexterity, eye-hand coordination, physical stamina, and strong mechanical ability.

Technical schools also prepare students for professional certification exams. In the electronics industry, a popular certification that a technical school can prepare its students for is the CompTIA A+ Certification. This is an entry-level certification for computer service technicians. The exam is designed to certify the competency of entry-level PC computer service professionals in installing, maintaining, customizing, and operating personal computers.

CompTIA is a large trade group, founded in 1982 and made up of resellers, distributors, and manufacturers. It sets voluntary guidelines dealing with business ethics and professionalism, and is involved with many issues including product returns, warranty claims, and price protection.

Historically, A+ Certification was a lifetime certificate, but starting in 2011, the A+ certificate must be renewed every three years by retaking the A+ test.

The A+ exam contains situational, traditional, and identification types of questions. All of the questions are multiple choice, and there is only one answer for each question. The A+ exam is open to anybody, although it is designed to be taken by those with at least six months of job experience as service technicians. Since you'll be starting your business this is a great way to become familiar with some of the intricate work that you'll be studying.

Currently, A+ is the only major non-vendor-specific hardware certification available for Microsoft Windows–compatible computer systems and can be a valuable addition to your knowledge.

Vendor-Specific Certifications

There are several vendor-specific certifications that you may or may not qualify for, depending on the brand (or vendor) for which you wish to become certified.

Fortunately, there is a testing program that is open to the public that provides certifications on Apple hardware and software so an individual can become a Macintosh Certified Technician. Again, if you're choosing to go into the Apple niche of the repair field, this certification would be most valuable to you and your marketing plan.

You can visit Apple's website for details, buy the study guides online, study on your own time, and then schedule a test at a local Sylvan Prometric Testing Center. These are located around the country and offer professional certifications for Macintosh computer systems. There are fees involved, but they are minuscule compared to a traditional education at a college or technical school, and one can become a certified Mac technician within weeks if a rigid study habit is formed.

The Repair Technician Schedule

It's time to figure out how much time you'll be able to spend working on your new business. It's a balancing act between your personal life and business life; however, as you might imagine or will soon discover, the lines are vague for an owner/operator.

In a new business you'll want to consider the market that you're appealing to. Will it be mostly business customers? Or will you appeal to the general market? Your operating hours may make a difference in a sale, and in the beginning, most small businesses will want every sale possible. Even after all of the potential benefits of being a business owner, the bottom line is that you're in business to make money. Hopefully a lot of it.

In the service industry, it seems counterintuitive to make customers work around your schedule. There is a fine line, and eventually within your day you will want to "call it quits." The point is to pick business hours that work for your customers, then tailor your life schedule around them.

Be Flexible and Accommodating

I started my computer repair business initially being open 8:00 a.m. to 5:00 p.m. This is a typical workday, and since I was an owner, it seemed to make the most sense for me. In the beginning I had a partner, my cousin Kyle Baccus, and we would both work and alternate lunch schedules. This gave us the flexibility to remain open for the entire shift, which kept us open for nine hours a day.

I quickly found myself getting calls from customers who wanted to drop off or pick up their repaired devices "after work." Well that meant that I needed to stay until 6:00 or 7:00 p.m.—and I was happy to do so. I felt that my customers needed to work too and I didn't want them to be inconvenienced. As a struggling new business owner, I needed to make things easy for my customers, not difficult. Now, with enough employees, we operate seven days a week.

In the beginning it'll most likely be just you running your operation. This is the simplest and quickest way to get started. However, it puts all of the pressure on you to make sure that everything gets done. Ultimately this means that your schedule will be somewhat dictated by the number of repair requests you have and the number of service calls you accept. I was personally of the mindset that I wouldn't turn down any customer unless the service request was way out of my depth.

My philosophy on the subject was that in the beginning, I didn't have a recognizable brand or a steady stream of business and I didn't have a reputation that I could lean on. All I had was my word and my promise to my customers. I regarded each of them as a potential "good review" somewhere on the Internet, in a coffeehouse, or at the family dinner table, so I made sure to attend to each new customer with a committed customer service mentality. Adopting this attitude ultimately means that your schedule will need to be flexible. It means that you'll need to be available, and if you are the good reviews and word of mouth will spread.

Don't plan on being able to work 8:00 a.m. to 5:00 p.m. Plan on working until the job is finished, then you can fall asleep knowing that your day is complete. Otherwise you may get complacent, figure that "there's always tomorrow," and find yourself in a bind if you are busier "tomorrow" than today. It's called the "snowball effect" because as your days flow from one to the next, your backlog of business gets bigger and bigger. This may seem good on the surface but it will backfire on you sooner or later as you will be fighting fires, making excuses to customers, and ultimately losing business. Remember the customer service factor? It's applies to your business 100 percent of the time!

Find a Niche: PCs? Macs? Tablets?

As you gather more information about how and when you will begin your new business, you may at first think about doing it all. This is a noble thought. However, you might soon be overwhelmed by the huge variety and intricate details of modern-day electronics and you'll find you can't even get your business off the ground.

The concept of a home-based computer repair business brings a broad range of services to mind. Let's discuss a few different fields of electronics that have a real demand for service—specifically in what I call the "handheld" device market. It consists of anything that a consumer can hold in his hand, and this simple action makes the necessity for service almost guaranteed. Remember Murphy's law . . . if something can go wrong, it will. In the case of consumers, if it can be dropped, it will be.

Provide a Solution to a Problem

I had some experience repairing iPods on the side. As you probably know, the iPod is an Apple, Inc. product and before I began my repair business, I did a little research on the manufacturer warranty and what customers needed to do if they ever dropped their device or cracked their screen.

This led me to a local Apple store, where I spoke to the customer service representatives about repair policies and what they were authorized to offer to customers with damaged iPods. I found that they were lacking—and that they only provided high-priced repairs for "out-of-warranty" service requests, like cracked screens. I had friends who had iPods with cracked screens and I could see a fit here.

If I could provide a solution to this problem, I knew that I had a good, marketable idea. I bought a few iPods online and started to take them apart. I found that they could be repaired. My next task was to find the parts and begin my business. I knew I had a good idea, and I knew that I had a direction that I wanted to go in. I picked that Apple iPod market and my service business grew from there.

When it's dropped, it will need service. Who are they going to call? Hopefully you!

When contemplating your business, and while it's still in start-up mode, it's a great idea to focus on a niche. This gives you the ability to become the expert in a field and also focus your marketing efforts to concentrate on a specific market and master it. You will find that there is a lot of competition in the field, but competition is a good thing. It keeps the playing field level. It also gives your new business guidelines and structure from the beginning. Assess your competition, look at what they are doing right, and make it your goal to do it better.

Before you go off and start doing your market research, ask yourself if you have any skills that might make this process easy to start. Truthfully, you're going to want to make things easier on yourself, so why not take the time now to narrow your vision and look at a specific field that will make you happy, make you feel comfortable, and make you the most money.

Will it be the PC market? The Apple/Mac market? Maybe you'll just focus on tablets? Whatever your discipline, you're going to want to make an impression on the market. Remember, too, that even within the PC market you can fine-tune your business to specialize in desktop units or laptop units, even down to focusing on a specific manufacturer of each. Say, HP laptops.

Here are a couple of niches that you might find yourself thinking about. However, let's first define the two major types of home-based computers on the market. All home computers are "personal computers" or "PCs"—and this particular terminology is up for debate. For the sake of this discussion, we are going to break the "personal computer" market into two groups. I consider a "PC" to mean a computer that primarily runs the Windows operating system, and a Mac to run the Mac operating system. Bearing that in mind, where will your business begin?

PCs?

The PC industry celebrated its 35th anniversary in 2010. From its humble beginning in the form of hobby computer kits in 1975, the PC industry has come a long way. In 1975 fewer than 50,000 PCs were sold, with a total value of about $60 million.

Today's PCs are dramatically different from the massive, "room-sized" boxes that emerged in the earliest years of computing. By the 1970s, the hobbyist could buy unassembled PCs, also called "microcomputers," and program them for fun, but truthfully they could not perform many of the useful tasks that today's computers can. Users could do mathematical calculations and play simple games, but the novelty of the computer was its selling point. Today, hundreds of companies assemble and sell personal computers, useful software, and mind-blowing games. PCs are used for a wide range of functions, from basic word processing for writing documents (as I am doing as I write this book) to editing photos and videos to managing businesses. At home or work, PCs are an important piece of the world today and can do almost anything that you ask them to do; in fact, it's hard to imagine a world without them now.

With all of the different businesses that create, assemble, and distribute PCs, most of them are loaded with the most current copy of Microsoft Windows. In fact, Microsoft (owned by Bill Gates) was selling an average of 650,000 licenses each day in 2011 alone. That's a lot of computers, and a lot of potential customers for your new burgeoning business. How can a business owner like you capitalize on the PC market? The sheer number of computers in the market is a good indicator that there's business to be had.

However, all of the computer manufacturing competition out there drives the price of PCs down, and therefore makes them more "disposable" than ever before.

Keep in mind that the PC repair market is a fierce market and the small businesses that have made a success out of this industry are doing so in bulk repairs and services. As I said before, success is in numbers, so higher volumes and lower margins should be expected.

Macs?

By now you know a little about the "fruit company" called Apple, Inc. Apple makes Macintosh computers, or "Macs." In the late 1970s, Apple was just an emerging business that needed to deal with the success of PCs.

For the next two decades, Apple primarily manufactured personal computers, but it faced terrible sales and very low market shares through the 1990s. In 1996, Apple Computer, Inc. brought in Steve Jobs—making him CEO—and instilled a new corporate philosophy for delivering simple and effective designs to the market. This new direction was a turning point for the company.

By 2001, Apple developed the iPod. It seemed like an interesting direction at the time, to bring in a music player as a main product for the company. But it didn't play compact discs or cassette tapes. It played MP3 music files—MP3 music files that were downloaded by your Mac.

The combination of the iPod and the Mac has strengthened the Apple market in a way that seemed unimaginable. Apple, Inc. doubled its revenues from 2010 to 2011, and then again doubling in 2012, which has proven that the world wants Macs.

Since the Mac does not use the Windows operating system, this is a distinctly different line of computers for repair. There's no rule that says you can't specialize in both Macs and PCs, but since you're considering a niche, the Mac computer option is a strong one, especially if you have any Mac experience at this point.

Macs tend to be more expensive for customers to initially purchase, therefore they are more likely to maintain and keep the units repaired and operational. While there is a significantly lower number of Macs in the marketplace compared to PCs, the margins can be higher with each repair.

Tablets?

Tablets are making their way into households across the country, and many contend that the tablet market may overtake the computer market altogether in the future. There's a lure with a tablet that you just don't get with a computer, and the consumer market is buying tablets in huge volumes.

The tablet "computer" has made big strides in the last few years mainly because of Apple's invention of the iPad. The iPad is thin and has a touch screen that allows a customer to operate the device without a keyboard. These devices have exceptional web browsing capabilities and, unlike a computer, they have hundreds of thousands of specialized "apps" that can be downloaded and used by most age groups. Apps include everything from games to specialized word processors to virtual musical instruments, and typically the apps make use of the touch screen and its performance.

After the invention of the iPad, many manufacturers joined the tablet revolution and can vary in terms of power and operating system. Most tablets use a special operating system designed to make the most of the touch interface. The touch capability gives a tablet its "cool factor" and makes the device fun and simple to use.

Today's tablets have exceptional battery life and cameras that make the handheld device fully functioning on road trips as well as at home.

The key to the tablet's usability is the touch screen. Without a functioning touch screen, a customer has a useless piece of hardware. A business can make an entire living on repairing touch screens and diving deep into the tablet niche. Tablets aren't cheap, so repairs are viable, and at a good margin. Bear in mind that the tablet market can be a great business and the trend seems to going well for tablet sales.

Smartphones?

In 2005 Google was snatching up start-up companies with potential, and among them was an almost unheard of operating system producer called "Android."

In 2011, two hundred and fifty million Android products were activated, compared to the one hundred and four million iPads and iPhones activated by Apple, Inc. Most recently, three out of four phones purchased were on the Android platform. That breaks down to fifteen Android devices being sold every second. These two-hundred-dollar devices are almost as popular as Big Macs from McDonald's, which sell at a rate of seventeen every second.

Currently the Android market has the lion's share of the smartphone market, and there's most certainly a need for service and repair in this field. Parts sourcing is most difficult for these products, but if it were easy, everyone would do it.

Apple, Inc. also manufactures a popular smartphone called the iPhone. Yes, so popular that at the writing of this book, we have five of them in our household alone!

Like the iPad tablet, the iPhone uses a touch screen interface on which it's dependent. If the touch screen fails, then the iPhone needs service. There are many businesses that are trying to thrive in the iPhone and smartphone market in general. The business that succeeds in this market will be offering same-day and while-you-wait services to walk-in customers. Users cannot be without their phones for long, so speed will be the key to this high-margin business niche!

It's well known that over the next ten years the computer industry will prosper and thrive with two additional driving forces—consumer electronics devices built with computing platforms and mobile devices such as smartphones and multifunction cell phones.

Computer hardware and software platforms are invading fixed-function electronic devices in telecommunication, consumer electronics, auto electronics, and related industries. The long-term trend is clear: Most electronic devices will sooner or later be based on microprocessors, software, networking, and other computer hardware technologies. This will happen because consumers are drawn toward technology and as more products embrace and integrate microprocessors, the more the market for the electronics repair industry will grow. The key question is not if this will happen, but when it will happen in the various product segments.

Are you ready to take the next step?

There are a lot of things to consider as you make the decision to move into self-employment, and there are a lot of pieces to the puzzle. In the next chapter we'll get a good mental picture of your new endeavor. Keep an open, creative mind and soon you'll be open for business!

Envisioning the Business

Starting your own home-based computer repair business is your future. Kind of a scary thought, right? Ask yourself, "What do I picture? How will running this business fit into my life? What kind of changes must I make in order to allow this business, and my life outside of work, to become a balanced success?" Breaking down this huge and intimidating undertaking can make this daunting task much less scary and much more fun.

Begin with the end in mind. You are starting small with the opportunity for growth in your future. What is the name of your business, your logo, and your mission? What kind of business are you beginning? How will your customers find you? What are your hours of operation? These might seem like basic questions with easy answers, but these decisions are the heart of your business and your success, and you want to be sure you start on the right foot from the beginning. The sections in this chapter will help you make these important decisions while keeping many factors in mind.

Remember, this is your passion and your niche. You can do this. With the support of your family and trust in yourself and your business plan, you have the start to a great home-based business built by you. Ask lots of questions along the way, take good notes, talk out decisions with your most trusted advisers and family, and get excited about your new adventure!

Start-Up Considerations

The start-up of a business is the hardest part. There are some easy steps and then there are some difficult ones. I suggest that you start a checklist and knock off the items in order so you gain a sense of accomplishment as you move forward.

The first thing I think of when I say or hear the word "start-up" is: How much is this going to cost?

This is an important aspect of starting your business. You must have some capital to do so. Capital is money, or cash to be more specific. Additionally, you can use credit cards to help fund your business, but you won't be able to make every purchase you'll need on a credit card, so having funding in place is necessary.

That being said, you can start a business on a limited budget. The more cash you have, the more you can do in the beginning. However, there is nothing wrong with a limited-budget business start-up. In fact, it can be the smarter way to go. You limit your up-front risk, minimizing potential losses until you get established and truly know if the path you've chosen is right for you.

Live Lean and Hungry

So there I was, sitting at my kitchen table surrounded by ideas, checklists, and to-do charts. I wasn't making any income, but I had some savings and credit cards to use to my advantage. I could have easily given up, gotten depressed, and resorted to job hunting. Instead, I did a week's worth of research and found out that starting my own business was not as expensive as I had imagined.

Yes, if you imagine that you'll start your business and in a month be walking into a nice building with a retail front with several employees and a warehouse full of inventory, you're going to have to work fast and you had better have a ton of cash to boot. I was in a different frame of mind: get my enterprise started on my kitchen table and stay on my kitchen table until I knew that I could afford to upgrade my work environment.

In fact, this philosophy still holds true for me today. I run my businesses without debt attached to them. Basically, if I can't afford to do something, then I don't do it. This works for me and I like the feeling of not being over my head in debt.

So as I progressed down the self-employment path, I was able to success- fully begin my first business with less than $12,000 in combined cash and credit. After a few short years I have thirty-one employees and seemingly limitless growth potential in sight, but I continue to subscribe to the "If I can't afford it, I can't do it" principle.

However, there are factors and costs that cannot be avoided, so of course there's risk involved. If there weren't, then everyone would do it. The very thought of business ownership and moving on to the start-up phase of owning a business can be described as risky and that's great. Entrepreneurs are risk-takers and love the challenge!

It will be impossible for me to give you a cold, hard price on what it's going to cost to get your business up and running. All of us business owners do things a little differently.

So what can you expect as you need to pay for items that are part of your start-up? I'm going to assume that you don't have an endless supply of cash on hand. If you did, you might be reading a different book entitled *How to Buy an Island*. Since you're more likely in a scenario similar to the one I was in, let's get into the basics of what you'll need to begin, assuming that you have a desk, a chair, a filing cabinet, and a workbench. If not, add those to this start-up list!

A Lawyer

This can be an intimidating experience, but I strongly suggest that you retain a lawyer. This is for help now and in the long run, albeit it is an expensive part of the business. This will certainly be necessary if you identify more than one owner for the business, more specifically to say that if you plan to have a partner, because setting up the proper paperwork now can save each of you in the long run.

Your lawyer can also set up the legal business name and establish the articles of incorporation for you if you'd like. However, these items can also be done by you to save money, and we'll talk about that later.

Generally your attorney will give you good, sound legal advice and even provide an opinion on your new venture as it's in start-up phase. A seasoned business lawyer will have seen many examples of successful and failed businesses and will be able to shed some light on your scenario as you talk out your plan. Many lawyers are connected with banks and private investors, which can also benefit you in the future.

Lastly, having a lawyer who knows who you are, what you're trying to accomplish, and what the nature of your business will be can be very helpful. Even if you don't speak on a regular basis as your business takes off, if you ever need the assistance of someone who knows the law, you can call on "your lawyer" in the future.

Typical price for setting up your business paperwork: less than $1,000.

An Accountant

I also highly recommend meeting with a certified public accountant (CPA). This can simply be to help you determine how you want to structure your business for tax and accounting purposes. You do not need to have the accountant balance your books, write checks for your business, or even look into your bank account. Unless you understand accounting and tax regulations, it is a good idea to have an initial meeting with an accountant to help you get the books started off right.

In fact, use that initial meeting to decide whether or not that particular accountant seems to be a good fit for you in the future. As your business closes out each fiscal year, you will want a CPA to review your books and prepare your taxes for the IRS and the state in which you operate. I consider my CPA expense a "peace of mind policy," because working without one would be unsettling. I prefer to have the professionals help me when it comes to the IRS. I just think that it's a smart move.

Remember this: As you choose your CPA, look for personality compatibility. I found a CPA I really like; he understands my needs and doesn't belittle me or tell me that I'm doing things wrong. Instead, he will make suggestions that will correct my mistakes, which keeps me feeling confident that he's the right person for my business. Don't be afraid to take advice from your CPA regarding your books or taxes. It's his profession. If your CPA starts to offer advice on how to repair computers, maybe it's time to look for a replacement!

Typical price for a consultation: free to $250.

An Insurance Agent

At some point in the near future, you're going to need business insurance. Most people can obtain business liability and an entire supplemental menu of insurance options from their current personal insurance agent.

If your current insurance agent does not provide business insurance options, consider moving your personal insurance policies to one who does. Not only are insurance companies looking to provide you with personal, business, and life insurance, some of the bigger insurance carriers are also banks. That's right, your insurance agent might have a banking option and because of low overhead (no physical bank locations), the interest rates can be the best in the industry.

A Computer

You're going to need a computer, period.

There's no getting around today's technology, and in fact it is that very technology that will bring you a wealth of customers and business.

The fact is that you won't be able to do research or communicate in the way your customers will want to communicate with you if you don't have a computer. Computers are very accurate; they don't take lunch breaks and a computer hosting your website will work twenty-four hours a day.

Now you can use the old computer that you've been using to e-mail your friends for the last couple of years and that will likely get you by for a while. However, I suggest that you buy a new one. New technology. New software. Not one that's loaded up with the family pictures that your spouse may need to "borrow" as your business is operating.

Buying a new computer can be just the motivation that you need to make yourself feel important and ready for the new venture. There is a lot of discussion out there about which operating system (PC or Mac) is the best to run your business on a daily basis, and I have my own opinion on the matter. I suggest that you buy the system that suits your business, for example if you're going to be offering Mac repair, then you should be using a Mac.

Typical price for a new computer system with basic software: $500 to $1,200.

A Printer

As much as you think you don't need one, you will need a printer to print copies of documentation from time to time. Your printer can be simple and practical or extravagant and over the top. Whichever way you go, make sure it prints in black and white and on 8.5" by 11" paper. I'm being a little sarcastic when I say this—all printers that you'll find for sale should have this capability. I suggest a simple laser printer for now, as it's all that you will need.

Typical price for a new laser printer: $150 to $300.

A Website

You might get tired of hearing me talk about your website in this book. The reason that it comes up so often is because you must have one, even if it's a simple one-pager, describing your business, with your telephone number and address. The fact is that some customers will do research on you, and the only place people research things these days is on the Internet. You want them to find you there.

Your website will be a large part of your marketing scheme and can greatly increase your customer awareness and reach. Don't know much about websites? Don't know anything at all? There are companies that will do all of the work for you, but if you're going into the computer repair business then you probably have a little bit of technological smarts.

Find an e-commerce website solution that provides you with templates, backgrounds, and the framework for a website. From there, you take your "whiz kid" attitude and make the premade template your own. Your site will end up being hosted offsite and in a secure location; this is good. The last thing you need to think about now is buying a second computer, learning HTML or some other form of Internet language, and scripting a website from scratch. That can take a very long time in comparison.

Typical price for setting up your website with an e-commerce provider: less than $300, plus monthly fees.

Office Supplies

You can do a lot of what you need to do on the keyboard of your computer, but you'll really need to buy a few office supplies: notepads, pens, and paper to start.

Also think about your filing system. You have the filing cabinets, correct? You'll need a few hanging folders and a box of file folders. Keep all of those business papers organized and in your filing cabinet! This is a touchy thing for some people I know (me), but once you get organized, it makes your life so much more, well, organized.

Don't forget toner for that printer.

The necessary office supplies to get you started: $200 to $400.

A Telephone

There are a lot options when it comes to what kind of phone to buy. Do you use your cell phone as your office phone? Do you get a phone system? VoIP, hard line, cell tower, argh!

A great argument can be made for using a cell phone as the business phone, especially in the beginning. Chances are you already have a cell phone. I find, however, that keeping my cell phone for private use suits my lifestyle better and keeps me sane when it comes to my cell phone ringing. For example, you might be closed for business at 5:00 p.m., but your cell phone rings at 6:00 p.m. when you're out to dinner. You answer the call only to realize that it's a customer who wants to know more about your business, place an order, check on the status of a repair order, and so forth. Taking a business call while on personal time can get cumbersome.

So let's move on to a "professional" solution. There have been many advances in phone systems and the way businesses use telephone service these days. Within the last five years, I have personally moved all of my business phone services over to VoIP (Voice over Internet Protocol) service, and it's a perfect solution. We will talk a little more about VoIP later, but a new business owner can have a professional handset with auto-attendants, call queues, and all the features of a "big business" system for a simple monthly fee per phone. You'll just plug it into your Internet connection or local network and like magic you're conducting business over the Internet.

Typical price for a single VoIP phone with service: $50 to $75 per month.

Internet Service

With all this talk of computers, phones, and websites, you will have to have Internet service where your office is. This can be a simple cable modem to a broadband T1 line, but for now you will find that DSL or cable Internet service will provide you all of the bandwidth you'll need to get the ball rolling.

You will find that when you move into a commercial location from your home office, there can be a vast difference in Internet capabilities. Specifically, commercial locations typically have faster options. For now, you can thrive on home-based services.

Typical price for Internet service (varies by region): $50 to $110 per month.

Tools

You can't have a computer repair shop and use the tools you have in the garage to work on your 1986 Chevy pickup. No, you will need a set of specialized tools that will allow you to open, rework, and reassemble computers, phones, tablets, or whatever line of devices you choose, and each has a specific toolset.

Typical toolset for basic computer repair needs (adding tools as you expand your service line): $100 to $150.

Inventory

Inventory is important and can also be the most costly part of your start-up as most business owners get excited and overbuy what they plan to sell.

I like to take a different approach. I prefer to make a sale, then buy the inventory in the beginning. It does slow things down a bit, but I warn my customer that the part "needs to be ordered" or is "out of stock," then I set the expectation that it might take a day or two to get things rolling. This is why I choose to diagnose and call customers the same day that I receive their device in for repair, so that if I do need to buy a part for their unit, I can place an order and typically have it the next day. Another option would be to visit a local supply store each afternoon and pick up parts yourself.

So with this "Just in Time" (JIT) inventory system in play, you can balance your cash with your sales more closely and not overbuy inventory up front. You will be sorely disappointed if you make a large purchase of 750 gigabyte hard drives thinking "I'm going to install a lot of these," only to have them sit on your shelf for six months as technology increases, prices decrease, and you can't get rid of them. That's "bad" inventory and you don't want that.

I say buy a few items that you might need. Some memory, a few different-size hard drives, maybe even a broken computer from eBay for parts, and keep your inventory to a minimum until you see some real sales trends and know where you need to spend your money.

Start-up inventory: less than $1,000.

Sole Proprietorship, Partnership, or Corporation

This can be a difficult decision to make in the beginning, and as usual you should trust your lawyer and accountant to help you make this decision properly.

You might have a partner in mind. I did. I knew that I wanted a partner to work with me and to complement my strengths and assist me with my weaknesses. I wavered back and forth on whether or not to have a partner, but I decided having two heads was better than one, and having a partner can make the decision-making process easier at times.

In a sole proprietorship or a partnership, the owners are personally responsible for business debts. If the assets of the sole proprietorship or partnership cannot satisfy the debt, creditors can go after each owner's personal bank account, house, etc., to make up the difference. On the other hand, if a corporation runs out of funds, its owners are usually not liable.

The good news is that sole proprietorships and partnerships cost less to establish and they have minimal formalities. Corporations cost more to set up and run than a sole proprietorship or partnership. For example, there are the initial formation fees, filing fees, and annual state fees. Additionally, a corporation can only be created by filing legal documents with the state and must adhere to formalities. These formalities include holding director and shareholder meetings, recording corporate minutes, and having the board of directors approve major business transactions. If these formalities are not maintained, the shareholders risk losing their personal liability protection. While keeping corporate formalities is not difficult, it can be time-consuming.

Please note that under certain circumstances, an individual corporate shareholder may be liable for corporate debts, if, for example, a shareholder personally guarantees a corporate debt. Also, under certain circumstances, a court may determine that justice requires disregarding the corporate form and treating the acts and liabilities of a corporation as the acts and liabilities of the shareholders.

On the other hand, a sole proprietorship or partnership can open and operate with minimal formal documents to remain legitimate. Bearing all of this in mind, there are a lot of tax ramifications, legal information, and decisions to consider when choosing to go about this business on your own, with a partner, or as a corporation. Once again it's advisable to seek professional counsel on these matters. You want the structure of your business to be right, legal, and working in your best interest.

Naming Your Business

One of the most exciting parts about starting your own business can be naming your business—and it's also required. For you to legally own and operate a business you must secure a name that is not in use by another business and then properly make it your own. There are different ways to go about this.

First, you're going to want to come up with several name ideas to give yourself some options, and don't get too excited about a particular name or start advertising your business under a particular name until the paperwork is done, you have a registered employer identification number (EIN), and you have completed the articles of incorporation (if starting up as an LLC). Until you complete these items, you do not own the rights to your name! Just imagine if you had an established business and some new company started using your name to operate. You wouldn't stand for it. Neither will anyone else, so make sure you're not treading on another business's good name and come up with something unique.

Simultaneously, you're going to want to start looking at Internet domain names if you're going to start a website. I say "if" you're going to start a website, but truthfully this is not an option in today's Internet-based world. The fact is that you will need a

Capitalize on an Existing Business

Have you ever considered buying a business that is already up, running, and making a profit? Or maybe not making a profit but you can find the weakness and turn it around? Consider looking for an established business to buy. The business-buying game can be a tricky one, however, as in real estate, you may land on some great deals and take advantage of a softened market. If you have the cash to go down the business-buying path, it might the quickest way to get into self-employment.

website to operate your business even on a small scale. Businesses without a website that provides hours, services, prices, and the ability to make a sale online quite frankly limit their exposure and limit their ability to be successful.

This game of coming up with a name that is available, both in your state and on the Internet, can prove to be challenging. For example, you may want to call your business "Ryan's Computer Repair." You do a search to see if this name is available for use and then you can proceed. Don't be surprised if simple names like "Computer Repair," or even variations on names like "MicroCom" are unavailable. Remember you're competing with the entire country for a unique name . . . and with regard to your domain name, you're competing with the entire world.

Make It Legal

Applying for an EIN is a free service offered by the Internal Revenue Service. The IRS says to beware of websites on the Internet that charge for this free service. While there are services that provide a complete solution and will complete this for you to ensure that you are making the correct decisions when creating your new EIN, it is a task that can be completed by you. There are several options according to the IRS website to register your EIN:

- Apply Online. The Internet EIN application is the preferred method for customers to apply for and obtain an EIN. Once the application is completed, the information is validated during the online session, and an EIN is issued immediately. The online application process is available for all entities whose principal business, office, agency, or legal residence (in the case of an individual), is located in the United States or US Territories. The principal officer, general partner, grantor, owner, trustor etc. must have a valid taxpayer identification number (Social Security number, employer identification number, or individual taxpayer identification number) in order to use the online application.
- Apply by EIN Toll-Free Telephone Service. Taxpayers can obtain an EIN immediately by calling the Business & Specialty Tax Line at (800) 829-4933. The hours of operation are 7:00 a.m. to 7:00 p.m. local time, Monday through Friday. A representative takes the information, assigns the EIN, and provides the number to an authorized individual over the telephone. Note: International applicants must call (267) 941-1099 (not a toll-free number).

- Apply by Fax. Taxpayers can fax a completed Form SS-4 application to their state fax number (see the website for your state's fax number) after ensuring that the Form SS-4 contains all of the required information. If it is determined that the entity needs a new EIN, one will be assigned using the appropriate procedures for the entity type. If the taxpayer's fax number is provided, a fax will be sent back with the EIN within four business days.
- Apply by Mail. The processing timeframe for an EIN application received by mail is four weeks. Ensure that the Form SS-4 contains all of the required information. If it is determined that the entity needs a new EIN, one will be assigned using the appropriate procedures for the entity type and mailed to the taxpayer. Find out where to mail Form SS-4 from the second page of the form.

I prefer to visit www.irs.gov on the Internet. This is where you'll want to start your paperwork and first register your EIN. According to the IRS website, you need an EIN if you:

- Started a new business
- Hired or will hire employees, including household employees
- Opened a bank account that requires an EIN for banking purposes
- Changed the legal character or ownership of your organization (for example, you incorporated a sole proprietorship or form a partnership)
- Purchased a going business
- Created a trust
- Created a pension plan as a plan administrator
- Are a foreign person and need an EIN to comply with IRS withholding regulations
- Are a withholding agent for taxes on non-wage income paid to an alien (such as an individual, a corporation, or a partnership)
- Are a state or local agency
- Are a federal government unit or agency
- Formed a corporation
- Formed a partnership
- Administer an estate formed as a result of a person's death
- Represent an estate that operates a business after the owner's death

Since the very first item on their bulleted list is "started a new business," this is the very first thing you should consider doing on your road to being self-employed. Registering and obtaining your name quickly is important. At this stage you will need to divulge the type of business, whether it be a sole proprietorship, partnership, LLC, or other type of business. It's a good idea to have had a meeting with your lawyer and accountant before you make any decisions as to the structure of the business that might be costly to correct later.

This is some of the real work required to get a business off of the ground. Most people don't have the knowledge it takes to get things moving and therefore countless small businesses never get off the ground because of obstacles like registering an EIN. Since you're taking the path to self-success, forge forward and you'll find that the process is much easier than you expected, and that obtaining your EIN is rewarding and relatively instantaneous. Once it's registered to you, it's yours.

Finding a Domain Name

So it's time to make a decision—you need a domain name that relates to your business name. You may have something clever in mind, but you're going to want a domain name to go with that catchy business name that you've registered with the IRS, and ideally these will match for several helpful reasons.

First, if you want to be found on the Internet, you have to have a website. If you have a website, you have to have a domain name. For example, Google's domain name is Google.com.

Your domain name will carry throughout your entire business marketing plan and will be key to creating a brand that will stick in your customers' minds. The tricky part will be aligning your business name with your domain name, so act fast and lock down your decision! There are domain-name registrars, and typically a domain name can be secured for less than $10 per year, if it's available. If you don't have any experience with domain names, you might find it difficult to come up with something that's not already taken.

Spend some time checking with a registrar and searching for available domain names online. You can also type a potential name into your web browser's search bar and find that there's no website behind it, or that there's an error message. This doesn't necessarily mean that the name is available. Here are some possibilities:

1. The domain name is available.

2. The owner is designing the site but hasn't posted it yet.
3. The owner purchased the name for future use.
4. The owner bought the name, hoping to resell it at a profit.

Unless you get lucky or have a unique domain name, you will most likely spend some time finding the perfect available match. This is step one to starting your business entity, and the key is to remember that this is a difficult thing to change in the future so don't pick something that's limiting or that ties the business to one particular product. Basically, you want a name with these characteristics:

■ A Short Name. The maximum allowed size is sixty-three characters, but keep the name as short as possible. That's easier to type and remember for your customers.
■ A Memorable Name. Names with special characters like hyphens and underscores are harder to describe to customers over the phone. Visitors aren't as used to them either and you may inadvertently send customers to your competitors if they have similar names without special characters.
■ A Descriptive Name. Use your company name or a description of your service instead of company initials. People would instantly know what a site called "www.WorkFromHome.com" is generally about (although they might be suspicious). The full title is much more descriptive than the acronym "WFH.com."

Just remember that most web hosting companies and domain registrars let you check the availability of a domain name and its associated extensions (like .com or .org). Some even offer alternate versions if the name you searched for is not available.

While you're at it, this is a good time to also get your blog created. What is a blog, you might ask? A blog, short for "web log," is simply a discussion by you on an information site that resides on the Internet. You may not think that blogging is right for you; however, I still highly encourage you to secure a blog domain name that matches the domain name you're using to operate. For example, your domain name may end up being www.ryanscomputerrepair.com, so you should try to secure blog.ryanscomputerrepair.com. You can register the domain name for your blog through a blog-registration site like Wordpress.com or Blogger.com. Still not convinced? Wait to read more about blogging later—you'll become a writer before you know it.

Now that you've got your domain name, what do you do next? There are entire businesses devoted to making websites and determining which style of website is the best. Unless you have experience in making websites or are willing to learn an entire trade in addition to your current new venture, I recommend that you find a service or a template that you can begin with and expand on.

Most domain-name registrars offer domain-name hosting services, website-building services, e-mail hosting, and other important website functions. Additionally, there are entire businesses that offer complete "e-commerce" solutions that bring you a world of options and opportunities that have very little or no up-front cost. There are pros and cons to each option, but simplicity might be the key, especially in the beginning.

Most e-commerce solution sites have a common theme. Every e-commerce website wants to sell, and many are successful. If you go with an e-commerce service you'll want to find a solution that can craft a unique website to meet your specific needs.

A well-tailored e-commerce solution can bring you the following:

- A well-strategized website solution
- An experienced team of knowledgeable webmasters
- Internet marketing and search engine optimization
- Website templates, design, and development
- A shopping cart
- Third-party application integration
- Twenty-four-hour support and site maintenance
- E-commerce hosting with nightly backups and redundant systems

Successful e-commerce solutions require clear goals from you, the owner, which in turn means precise planning and a partner in the e-commerce world who can analyze your needs and turn them into the face of your business on the Internet.

If you get your information and your goals lined up in an orderly fashion, you too can have an operating website taking orders for you at all hours of the day.

Designing a Logo

As part of your start-up activities, you're also going to want a logo that represents your new computer repair business. A logo is a graphic that symbolizes your brand and your business. It helps distinguish your business from others. It is essential to your business to come up with a unique, eye-catching, and attractive logo because it's your symbol—your coat of arms—and it will remind the public of what you are. It is part of the entire identity of your business.

Don't put the cart ahead of the horse—for a logo to be made you're going to need an established business. Many logos end up being initials or part of the business name, so designing a logo before you have a registered name might prove to be a waste of work or finances.

Know that most consumers in the market rely on their sense of sight while shopping and your logo is a way for people to notice who you are. Your logo is your frontline representative and will remind people about your business whether they are on the road, watching TV, reading a newspaper, or searching the Internet. Once you're established and your logo is well known, it is your brand as it communicates your image and your appeal!

Additionally, it's a way for your customers to remember you more easily. Remember that there's a sea of burgeoning businesses out there, and keeping your business in the forefront of the consumer's mind is ideal. A familiar logo is like seeing an old friend, as your customers will relate your logo to your high-quality services—this will enhance the customer's view of your business and keep you ahead of the competition.

That being said, unless you have some graphics knowledge you might want to outsource your logo design to a professional. The benefits of having a consultant design and build your logo is that typically you can collaborate with a designer and receive multiple drafts until an amazing logo, to your liking, is complete. A freelance or other professional logo designer will provide you with many styles, sizes, and electronic file formats of your new logo as well, which is helpful when building your website all the way down to ordering business cards. Having your logo available in many sizes is key.

Customer Service Is Key

As I am starting my businesses, I typically take my potential customer's perspective in mind. This begins from deciding on a business name all the way to the opening day. There is a component to customer service that I never really understood or even contemplated until I saw it happen at my own business—and that is enjoying natural, repeat, and word-of-mouth business down the road.

It's an amazing thing, taking care of your customers. You will have some customers who will find fault with you, no matter who's to blame, what the fault is, and even if you did everything right. It's a difficult position to be put in when you know, as the business owner, that you've provided great service, but then some detail gets thrown into the works that causes an issue between you and your customer. Truthfully, a successful business is one that deals with customer-service issues correctly and capitalizes on good customer service in the future.

My goal, when dealing with my customers, is to treat them as I would expect to be treated. I don't want to be intimidated into making a purchase. I want to be greeted when I walk into a business, and I love being called by my first name when I'm about to spend some money.

Unfortunately in the service industry there's a stigma that surrounds the "repairman" in any industry—and customers can be wary. Have you ever taken your car to a mechanic and found yourself thinking "OK, let's see what this is going to cost me" or worse, received an estimate for parts that you didn't think needed to be replaced?

Try to remember that as a service provider you may experience some of these negative reactions from your customers as you quote them prices and service their expensive electronics. You can combat this easily with good communication and good customer service. Since you're going to be operating a legitimate, long-term computer repair business, it's in your best interest to start with your very first sale and make it an amazing experience for your customer. An amazing experience can simply be doing what you say you'll do.

Think about it. Do what you say you'll do.

If you take service orders and tell the customers "I'll call you tomorrow with an estimate," you will need to call those customers by the stated time or earlier. They will appreciate you for it and they will trust you. In turn, they will be more willing to work with you, give you their money, and come back in the future.

Remember how I said that I never really understood how repeat business would affect me? Well, after several years of providing high-quality goods and services to my customers, they told their friends about what an amazing business I had, and their friends started showing up. Those people told other people. I realized that I was gathering more customers than ever before, yet my marketing budget was not increasing. That's word-of-mouth advertising working for you. While traditional marketing ideas can quickly drain your bank account, word-of-mouth advertising is free, and word-of-mouth advertising is spread because you provided good service, you were trustworthy, and you did what you said you would do, period.

The Difference Between Amateur & Professional Home-Based Repairs

A repair is a repair, right? Well, actually there are a number of differences that can make you a professional in your field versus an amateur.

Just like the sports arena, there are amateur teams and there are professional teams. There is nothing wrong with being an amateur athlete. In fact, it's quite an accomplishment. Not everyone can be an athlete and it takes a certain type of person to be good enough for amateur status.

For example, a college-level athlete. Once the collegiate-level athlete progresses and moves up the ranks he may opt to go professional. Like college athletics to professional athletics, the computer repair game can be divided into these categories as well. The professional service company possesses stricter rules to which you, the business owner, must adhere to. But as in athletics, there's a huge difference in the moneymaking capability between the ranks.

Amateur repairs are services provided to friends and family as favors or as gifts, and typically an amateur will not charge for services or will possibly charge a nominal amount for the work performed.

At the professional level, services are provided at a cost and in return the customer expects a warranty, support, and that a company that will be available for support in the future. Professional businesses are the only successful businesses that survive in the real world. While you might be thinking "I can do this on the side," be forewarned that your business will never bring you the satisfaction and true financial freedom that you are dreaming about.

If your dream is to be a football player, then your dream is to be in the NFL making professional wages and being the star of the game. If your dream is to be a business owner, then your dream is to provide high-quality services and support at your business, make professional wages, and be the star of the industry.

Amateur Repairs

I see the need for someone to provide amateur repairs on a small scale. For example, repairing one's own devices if the need ever arises. These can be done cheaply and on the fly, but in America, there's no room for "under the table" services and sales. There are far too many consequences for business owners to try to run "under the table," "cash only," or "under the radar" when it comes to the IRS and state governments. It is difficult for a small business to operate in the US due to the laws that business owners must abide by, and rules that we need to follow. There are taxes to pay. A business owner must understand that these taxes and laws are merely part of the cost of running a business—a professional business.

Professional Repairs

You will find that the demand for professional computer services and repairs is great. The reason being is that a truly professional business will provide value-added benefits that offer trust and peace of mind to the customer. In my mind, these benefits are actually more like necessities but will commonly be overlooked by the amateur businessperson.

Honesty

One of the first virtues of a professional business is being honest. Telling your customers that you will do something, and then doing it, will carry you to the finish line. Be up front with your customers—don't lie. If you're caught in a lie, you're sunk. Be honest and in your case as you start up a business don't be afraid to say that you're "new." It's a good way to begin a relationship with a customer and you might find that your eagerness and openness will start the flow of customers.

Accessibility

Your accessibility will be a key factor in determining your status as a professional. Hopefully, you'll have stated business hours and you will answer your business telephone when it rings during those hours. Personally, when I call a small business during their stated business hours and get an answering machine, it doesn't make me feel that they care about me or their business.

There are some excuses for not answering the phone; however, those anomalies should be stated confidently on a temporary answering machine recording. If you can't get your repairs completed while being available to answer incoming telephone

Establish Yourself in the Market . . . As Yourself

There I was, running my computer service business, and everything seemed to be moving along fine and at a pace I could enjoy. I was hiring new employees, about one every other month, and I was able to keep my local presence and Internet presence in check with one another. In fact, I started seeing some repeat business from local referrals and my walk-in traffic was increasing.

I was soon able to run TV commercials, which really sped up my phone traffic and sales.

Then one day a customer came into our service location and said, "I need to speak to Ryan Arter, the owner." I was paged by our customer service department and was told about my visitor.

When I greeted her she said, "No, I need to see the owner, Ryan Arter." I stated that I was the owner, and that I was Ryan Arter.

She described a completely different person from me, someone I had never seen before. She said that she found us on Craigslist.com advertising iPhone repairs, and that she responded to the ad and spoke to a gentleman who agreed to meet her at a local coffee shop to perform her needed repair.

She then followed up with a story that was almost too funny to believe. This gentleman announced himself as Ryan Arter from Mission Repair, and said that he would typically meet his customers at coffee shops to take care of their problems. I asked her if she was able to obtain a business card from the gentleman. She did not have one. I also asked for a copy of her receipt. She did not get one. I asked her if she had any documentation from this mysterious clone of myself, and she said that she happened to snap a picture of him while sitting across from him after her repair was complete. I looked at the picture and I didn't recognize the person whatsoever!

As it turns out, this guy was impersonating me and my business. The tragic part about the story was that she was continuing to have a problem with her phone after the repair, which is why she came into our location looking for me, and a resolution.

I was able to get her to realize that she had been lied to and that she gave her money to someone I did not endorse or have an affiliation with. It was an amateur who was using my good name and reputation to market and sell some kind of junk service from a booth at a restaurant.

In the end, I felt so terrible for this customer that I took care of her issues as a kind gesture. I was also able to give her a receipt, a warranty, a business card, and a coupon for her next repair if ever needed. Why did I do all of that? Because I am a professional.

calls, then it might be time to hire a customer-service representative! Until then, be accessible to your customer if you want to offer professional services.

Competitive Price

Being price-competitive is necessary; however, this doesn't mean that a business needs to offer the lowest price. Being competitive keeps everyone honest. If you can't be competitive in the market on a certain product or service then you may decide that it's not the product or service for you to provide.

There's an old adage that states, "You get what you pay for." Professional services cost more than nonprofessional ones. You may find that amateurs can undercut your prices and garner some customers, but they will ultimately fail because they will not have the means to support their customers in the future. Be competitive and keep your business trustworthy.

Quality Control

This is a big one. Each service that you perform should also come with a quality-control check. If you start your business as a one-person operation, you can still check the quality of your own work on a daily basis. If you've got two computers to service, repair one of them and set it aside. Repair the second one, and then move back the first. Grab your quality-control checklist. It should include a series of checkboxes that are designed for your product to ensure that you checked everything after a repair is done, including functionality, assembly, and cleanliness.

By taking time off from that first repair, when you come back to it, you can give it a fresh look and maybe find flaws in your workmanship that you didn't see before.

Apply Your Related Work Experience

I first learned about quality control when I was working in the corporate world, managing a large volume of computer repairs that were being performed by a large number of technicians. When I stepped into this role, the business did not have a quality-control team, department, or procedures in place. Like many businesses, I was at the mercy of a budget and there was no room in it to hire an additional team.

I ran a few reports to see what our warranty rate was at the time, and it was high. I felt that the warranty rate, also known as the RMA rate (RMA stands for "return materials authorization") could be lowered by implementing a quality-control check on each repair as it was being completed. As I interviewed the technicians about this, I received a lot of excuses and whining about the extra work, because I was going to have them perform the quality check.

In fact, I was going to have each technician perform a quality-control check on a different assigned technician's repairs. This kept them honest with their work. As it turned out, employees don't want to be called out by their peers, so the technicians stepped up their game and really took interest in making sure that each device was properly repaired and ready for inspection.

This lead to a decrease in RMA rate by over 8 percent, which in turn led to a bigger budget for me and my department, as well as a bigger profits for the business owner.

Checking your own work by offering a quality control inspection can take some time, but will pay back hugely in the long run. There's nothing worse than talking to customers, selling them a repair, performing the repair then delivering it back to them only to find that you forgot to put the screws in the case. It doesn't build confidence. Take the time to perform a quality check (and advertise that you do!) and you'll add to the professionalism of your business.

Receipt

Each customer who receives a product or service from your business should receive a receipt. This can be either a paper receipt or one that is sent electronically via e-mail.

A receipt will show the customer's information, the date in which a service was performed, what specific service was performed, and the price paid. The receipt (also called an invoice) can be a good place to convey additional information to your clients such as warranty terms, return policies, and so forth. You can also use your receipt as a marketing tool by adding a coupon or discount on the next repair.

Warranty

What is a warranty? A warranty is a statement from your business that guarantees that the service you provided and the part(s) that you installed will work and perform in the manner specified for a certain length of time. Warranties exist on just about every item that is manufactured, from small electronics to homes and cars. You will also dictate the extent to which the warranty applies.

Since your business will be a service business, keep in mind that the warranty you provide will most likely be a "parts and labor" agreement that gives the customer a reliable fallback in the event of an issue with your work. You will stand behind your work, right? I wouldn't use a service that didn't stand behind its work—it would make me feel too uneasy.

After-Repair Support

Once a repair is performed and a device is delivered back to a customer, this doesn't mean that the job is done. A professional business will have a means of contact, such as an e-mail address or telephone number, that will be available to the customer in the event that support is needed.

There will be countless times when a customer is happy with a service provided but will need to speak to someone about a repair or ask questions as a follow-up. A professional business will perform this support function as a basic customer service necessity.

Documentation

A percentage of your customers will undoubtedly call you back in the future. This may be for warranty work, to ask a support question, or to place another order with you. Your order database, which we will talk about later in the book, will keep all of the documentation on hand and facilitate any of these activities.

Imagine a customer calling back in a year asking to place another order for a second computer repair. You look the person up in your database, rattle off billing and shipping addresses (asking for any changes), verify the phone number, and then proceed with taking the new order. Being "in the system" will impress the customer, who will feel that you care enough to keep these details handy. Keeping a good, clean database will make life easier, so remember to keep that documentation current and correct.

Family Support

Your family's support in the endeavor will be a major consideration, especially during the first few months of business. There may be school schedules to consider, daycare pickup, and other daily life activities that you'll want to blend into your home-office business engagements.

Consider the "professionalism" of hearing a crying baby in the background when you're on the phone with a potential client. Without question, you're going to want to maintain a professional atmosphere at all times and call on your family support mechanism to assist with your personal responsibilities.

1. Discuss the arrangements of your new work schedule with your significant other ahead of time. It's possible that you may agree to drop the kids at school each day, so plan that into your business and begin the day at 9:00 a.m. Having the freedom and the ability to concentrate on developing your business is a necessity.
2. Try to keep your business space separate from your personal space if you maintain a home office.
3. Plan to adhere to your stated business hours. Be available when your customers call during your normal business hours.

Having your family's support will go a long way to developing a professional and reputable business. This holds true whether you run your business out of your house or out of a commercial location, and knowing that you have your family on your side will provide invaluable comfort and peace of mind.

Remember, this is your office, the start to your very own business. Make it perfect. Make it exactly what you need in order to facilitate your very best decision making, customer service, and professional repairs. This space will look different for every business owner and will change over time. In the last handful of years, my office space has been modified half a dozen times. This change comes from the way I, and my business, have evolved. Growth can be a tricky thing. My advice: Continually prepare for it all of time. The first aspect this growth will affect is your office space.

Organization is key. You will find that there are certain materials and tools that you need all the time that should be at your fingertips. Other things you will need only once in a while. Organize these things. You will also find that you need space to spread out and complete each of the individual tasks that your home-based business will require of you. Identify and organize these spaces, too. What tools do you need at each "station"? Have you taken the necessary precautions to keep yourself, as well as the devices, safe and well cared for?

Yes, it's a lot to think about and prepare for. But remember, you are not alone. This section will guide you through the setup of your home office and provide you with questions to ponder and tips to help you look and feel successful. In addition, as you travel this journey of starting up your own home-based business, rest assured that you will find what works best for you and you will feel empowered to change the things that need to be changed to best fit your business and your mission.

The Perfect Space

I started my business on my kitchen table. Literally. That was a mistake. It seemed like a good place—it was large enough for a computer, my "to-do" checklist, my plans, and a telephone. However, I quickly realized how often my family used the kitchen table for everyday tasks. So much so that I needed to get away from the disruption of sliding my stuff around so that my kids could eat their cereal. It was a necessary move.

It was apparent to me that I needed a dedicated space for my business to operate, not a temporary space. So I broke this task up into two parts. I set a goal to have a dedicated home-based space. Then I set a goal to lease a completely new space, a commercial space, within six months of my grand opening.

The Home Space

The home space can be a tricky one, but it's going to be necessary to keep your sanity and keep your business organized. Ideally, you'll have an extra bedroom or an office room that you can occupy and seal off from the rest of the family environment. Think about your customers, and whether you're willing to bring them into your home for a sales visit, to pick up or drop off a repair, or to consult with you about a future repair. You can have your desk in the corner of your bedroom but it might be a bit embarrassing if you invite a client in there to conduct business.

A basement room is a great place to run your business, and many homes have "bonus rooms" that also may do the trick. Just know that clients don't like to walk in on a family argument, or the kids dancing in front of a television set that's turned up too high. Design and decorate a dedicated area for your home office. It can be simple but it should be quiet. If you don't have clients visit your home, then it's up to you. Just be sure and dodge that flying football and watch your shins as your children are driving around their remote-control car. If space within your home is difficult to come by, take it as a sign that you want to grow your business quickly so that you can afford a commercial space.

A Desk Space

Your office furniture need not be new or expensive, but it does need to fit in terms of aesthetics and it does need to do its job. It's best not to clutter your floor or walls with bookcases when a filing cabinet might just do the trick. Shelving is great. Since you'll be staring at your desk space on a daily basis, it would be nice to keep items up off of your desk and onto nice-looking shelves. Remove the "visual noise" so you can concentrate on your work. A critical component to the desk space is a comfortable office chair and a reasonably comfortable guest chair. Sitting in a chair that is too low or too high, does not have adequate back support, or is wobbly may not seem like a problem initially, but over time your body will react, and you will develop sore, stiff muscles. If you have clients visit you at your home for a consultation, you will want them to have their own chair.

Keep your spaces clean. Dedicate fifteen minutes at the end of each day to make sure you're ready for the next day's work. If you have clients coming into your office this is especially true. You don't want them wading through snowdrifts of crumpled-up paper. These should bother you as well. It can get hard to find a certain file if your space is cluttered, and if you have someone calling your business on your toll-free telephone number, remember that every minute wasted means that expenses are piling up.

Lighting will be necessary and if you're staring at a computer screen for any length of time you'll find that lighting is also important for your eyes. To determine the best placement of lighting, as well as the best type to use, think of how the room will be used. Overhead lights are always a good idea. In addition, you may want to add task lighting in several areas.

If you will work and write at a computer, you will probably want a small reading desk lamp next to your keyboard. This will enable you to make notes and write without straining your eyes or having to move to another part of the room.

LED lighting is clear and offers bright light, so it makes a great choice for home- or commercial-office lighting. It makes tasks such as reading and writing easier by throwing a strong light just where you need it. You may want to look into dimming switches too, as these bulbs can be dimmed as needed for when the natural lighting in the room changes from day to night. LED home lighting is a great advancement over traditional incandescent lights and it's becoming more popular. While a traditional incandescent bulb will light a room but burn out relatively quickly, a LED light works differently. The longer life of an LED bulb means less money spent on replacing bulbs, and it's more energy-efficient than a traditional incandescent light bulb, which equates to lower costs in the long run.

There is a huge market out there for the "home office" businessperson, with many temptations. Just remember that if you don't need it, don't purchase it. Sure, there are fancy printer/scanner/fax machines out there and I certainly agree that you're going to need one, but opt for a simple model, even a used model, until your business justifies the purchase of a new one. A business can get started on the right foot by not overspending to make your new office too extravagant.

A Technician Space

The technician space is one of my favorite spaces in my business. The technician space is simple. A drafting table, a garage shop table, or other sturdy solid-top table would work well. Aside from my personal desk, the technician space is where all of the magic happens. When I flip on the lights at my business, I love seeing the technician's spaces light up. It's like the heart of the business starts beating. When the tech space is full of devices for repair, you'll know that you're doing something right.

As with your desk space, probably one of the biggest necessities here is good lighting. As a technician working on computers or other small devices, you're constantly focusing and adjusting to different lighting scenarios. Lighting that is directly overhead, even just above your head, is good.

All of that good lighting is going to be shining down on the work surface. Just about any flat, desk-like surface is good as long as it's clean and stable. It should be covered with an ESD (electrostatic discharge) mat. Not only do you want to properly prepare for ESD issues but also the matting is a runner-like material that is nonabrasive and a good cushion for your sensitive electronics.

Power outlets will be an important factor here and most likely your home was not designed with numerous outlets and circuits for business activities. Plan on having this space, which is separate from your desk space, near power.

A Filing Space

One of the most tedious jobs within your small business will be filing. Paper documentation is a necessity and if the need ever arises to retrieve a paper file, you'll be ready if you've kept an immaculate filing system. Filing cabinets are as common as staplers in an office setting, and your home office is no different.

Keep copies of every client invoice, signed agreement, lease, utility bill, and other important documents. You can start with a simple, two-drawer filing cabinet at business launch.

A Receiving Space

Once you place an order for a part or two, you'll need a place to perform your receiving duties. This task, at a minimum, will involve verifying that you received the items that you ordered. Typically in business, a purchase order is made for accounting purposes. This is then transmitted to the vendor of choice who turns it into an order for shipment. Once that order ships and arrives at your doorstep, you'll need to receive it.

Electrostatic Discharge Precautions

Electrostatic discharge, or ESD, is defined as the sudden flow of electricity between two objects caused by contact. Basically, if you have lots of electricity built up and that electricity meets the technology you are working with, it could cause irreversible damage.

ESD can be caused in two different ways: static electricity or electrostatic induction. Static electricity happens when two materials are brought into contact and then separated. Electrostatic induction happens when an electrically charged object comes close to a conductive object. Either way it happens, ESD is never good for your equipment. The sudden power surge can severely damage anything you have that runs on electricity.

To prevent ESD, you must create what is called an electrostatic protective area (EPA). Use a good amount of common sense: keep all high-charged objects away from your equipment, keep anything conductive on the ground, release any discharge from yourself on a countertop or similar surface before working, and don't drag your feet across the rug if you're wearing socks without shoes.

Antistatic ESD wrist straps are a good way to keep any electric charge inside of yourself to a minimum. Insulate your workstation with materials that do not conduct electricity, such as wood, rubber, or plastic. Make sure all workers who are handling the equipment necessary for your business know about ESD and are aware of the preventive measures that can be taken. Even take note of the flooring that you're working on. Have you ever rubbed your feet along a carpet and noticed a small electric shock when touching a door handle? If you can avoid working on carpet that is ideal!

The bottom line is that ESD can damage the equipment you're repairing even further if you don't take the proper precautions against it. Don't make your job harder, or even impossible, simply by introducing electricity into the object you are working with. Many EPA materials and objects are inexpensive and easy to obtain.

"Receiving it" counts as the physical receipt of the package from your delivery carrier (i.e., you have it in your hands), then in turn it counts as the book receipt into your inventory system. A receiving space is just an area where you can collect the daily shipments of packages ordered so that they can be opened, inspected, counted, and input into your inventory database. You should keep handy:

1. A sharp box-cutting knife
2. A garbage can for excess packaging material
3. A notepad and pen or pencil

Open each box, remove the inventory, count it, and verify that you received the correct amounts of each part ordered. The use of the notepad can be especially helpful if you have a large order in front of you.

An Inventory Space

If you're going to be repairing computers, you're going to need parts in stock to do so. This doesn't mean that you're going to have every part for every product you service in stock every day, but you will end up with some inventory, and at a minimum you will need to store customer units in an area while the repair is within your control. An inventory space will work well for this.

Think of your inventory space as a sacred location within your business. Inventory is money wrapped up in products, and if you're storing customer units overnight, that's customer money wrapped up in a device. There's a lot of money in inventory, and it needs to be kept under control and not taken lightly. It will be easy to keep inventory and customer units separate and under control in the beginning, but once business starts pouring in it can quickly become a nightmare.

I suggest an upright, two-door lockable cabinet for these sacred items. Make sure that you keep good control over these components and customer units. You don't want the neighbor's daughter wandering in thinking that nifty iPad sitting on your desk is community property. If it's a customer unit and you've been entrusted with it, you need to keep it safe.

A Shipping Space

Mark my words, even if you are a local business with no intention of shipping out devices to customers all over the country, you will end up shipping something to someone more than once. I recommend that you create a small shipping space in the beginning to ensure that you're ready for this eventuality.

The shipping space in your new business can be simple. Truly, if you're not intending to ship out of your home office on a daily basis, there is no need for alarm. However, you will want to have a few supplies on hand to perform this task easily (see the checklist below).

Once you have a few supplies, shipping with the United States Post Office is easy online, and printable labels can be created instantaneously. The nice part about the USPS is that they will pick your packages up for free on a daily basis and you can most certainly consult your mail carrier for advice on shipping options. Additionally, you can sign up for accounts with UPS and FedEx if you want to offer different methods of shipping for your customers.

Shipping Station Checklist

☐	Tape gun.	This is a simple device that is manually operated and keeps a spool of two-inch packing tape ready and at your disposal.
☐	Several small boxes.	You'll want a few of each size box that you anticipate needing to ship devices back to customers.
☐	Box cutter or scissors.	
☐	Sharpie or other writing implements.	
☐	Clipboard.	To keep all of your orders organized.
☐	Packing material.	You can use old newspapers, bubble wrap, kraft paper, or Styrofoam peanuts.
☐	Address labels.	
☐	Packing-list envelopes.	These will contain a copy of your customer's receipt or original invoice placed on the outside of each shipment.
☐	Any specialty packing materials that might be needed.	

_____

_____

_____

Shipping Supplies

You're getting closer and closer to being able to start your home-based computer business. While it may not be practical when you are just starting out, shipping is something to consider once you have gotten to steady ground in your business.

Snail mail has been around for hundreds of years. It's simple to package something up, take it to the post office, and send it off to the destination of your choice. Shipping, as well as taking orders, from across the country is an excellent way to expand your business when you are ready for that stage.

To get started, you will need an account with a shipping company. Creating a FedEx or UPS account is as simple as visiting the website and filling out a form. Having a shipping company that you can rely on will make the shipping process much simpler and less stressful. Remember that shipping rates are negotiable and will also be driven by volume. While you might not get the best rates to start, it's a great idea to have a monthly meeting with your representative to address your growth needs and to also renegotiate better shipping rates as you expand. There's positivity in growing, and getting amazing shipping rates can make the difference between a winning company and an unprofitable one.

You will also need basic shipping supplies to start. Boxes are obviously a necessity; Uline (among other box companies) offers over 1,700 sizes. Most often, you can also buy tape and tape guns from the same companies you buy your boxes from. However, tape and tape guns are often sold at stores such as Staples or Office Depot, if you would rather go that route.

Last but not least, you will need shipping labels. Labels are completely necessary when shipping for a business. Tape guns and proper packaging tape are the first step, but labels give the package a professional feel. It also makes organization and information-keeping much simpler. You can create custom-made labels through many shipping companies, or if you give them enough business, FedEx or UPS may provide these for you, with the proper label-making software and a printer!

The supplies necessary for shipping are generally not very costly and are well worth the price to expand your business. Once your company's name spreads throughout the country, more and more people will be interested in ordering services from you from different locations, so you will want to be ready to assist, and your profits can only rise from there.

The Commercial Space

A commercial space is just that. In fact, remember talking about offering a "professional" repair? This is just the ticket to truly bring your business into the professional world. When I first started looking for commercial spaces, I didn't really know what I needed or what I was looking for but quickly found out what I could afford. When you make the move to a commercial unit, you will need everything that we've listed in the "home space" but most likely more of it.

In much of the United States, if you pay attention to the road signs, billboards, and notices on many buildings you'll see a lot of commercial space for rent. There are different types of commercial real estate.

If you've got the capital, there can be good investment value in buying a piece of land to develop and construct a commercial building for your business. Land itself is typically a great investment because as the old saying goes, "They aren't making any more of it." Buying land, building a building, and subsequently moving into that building will take a lot of money and time. You most likely won't have much of either, as did I when I started, so this was not an option for me.

Then there is the retail shopping center type of building. These typically will have good visibility from main streets and highways and allow large lit-up signs for your business around the building. It may be in the form of a strip mall, a stand-alone building, or inside a mall itself. A retail spot may sound ideal. It too, however, comes with a hefty price tag. You can lease a commercial retail spot, but many landlords require three-year leases, and since the price for a retail space is relatively very high, your move-in costs will be too. Typically, most leases require a deposit in the form of first and last month's rent in advance. This is not abnormal or aggressive on their part, but if your rent ends up being ten thousand dollars per month, you may need thirty thousand dollars just to be able to set foot inside. Also, the retail spot is designed to bring in retail foot traffic. This means that the fixturing, displays, counters, and signage will all need to be professionally built and installed. This can add significant costs to your start-up adventure.

I took a different route. I looked at an office building classified as a "light-industrial" type of space. It was within a row of other businesses and had a glass front. The landlord wouldn't allow a large sign to go out in front and it was on a dead-end street, so I contemplated the use of such a building.

It did, however, have a large roll-up door in the back that I envisioned being used by the pickup and delivery trucks, two premade offices, two bathrooms, a small kitchen area, and a larger warehouse area that had a concrete floor to help me with me ESD issues. I could envision technician benches lining the walls, bright lights, and having the ability to receive walk-in foot traffic in the very large reception area. On top of all of that, the rent was cheap in comparison to a retail space. In fact, it was about 80 percent less than a retail spot, it had a shorter lease, water and garbage were included in the price, and it was about eight miles from my home, which was a lucky break.

My goal was to move into a commercial space within six months of starting my business; I did it in two. Once I zeroed in on my new space and signed my lease, I was able to buy a used desk, slide it into one of the offices and begin setting up my business so that I could have customers visit me at my commercial (professional) location.

Consider Your Future Location

I've now been with the same landlord for over five years. I have expanded my light industrial office space by leasing the units to the right and left of my original space. With a little build-out, imagination, and luck, I've been able to grow my business while expanding its real estate footprint with the help of my modular building. Consider the future when you're looking at leasing a unit for your business. Is there room to grow? Will you need to move in a year?

My landlord and I have a fantastic relationship and I have proven that I can be a good, reliable tenant. This relationship is a great building block for my business as I can use the landlord as a good reference, and we are both willing to work together, assisting each other any way we can, to ensure we each have a long-term successful business.

Is there building ownership in the future for me? I'm sure there is, but right now my business is benefiting from renting as we continue to grow.

Business Telephone Service

So by now you might be wondering how customers are going to get a hold of you. Snail mail and e-mail are helpful, but there's certainly no better way for customers to reach you than via your telephone. With technology these days, there's no better time to explore the options for using your telephone for business.

For example, VoIP telephone service is a twenty-first-century invention. VoIP stands for "Voice over Internet Protocol" and is a technology that allows you to make voice calls using your own home Internet service instead the old technology of using an analog or "hard line." Most VoIP services are seamless in that you can call either other VoIP customers or analog customers without issue—this includes local, long distance, mobile, and overseas telephone numbers. This is of huge benefit to you, as VoIP telephone numbers generally come with a special VoIP telephone that can be configured with a plethora of great features!

VoIP works by transferring the digital signal from your Internet service into a telephone signal that can come through your home phone. You can make VoIP calls

A New Toll-Free Number!

A lot of new business owners spend a lot of time trying to find the "perfect" telephone number. You know the kind, "555-TECH" or some other abbreviation or acronym that helps spell your business out? While this sounds good, consider today's technology.

If you market your new "555-TECH" telephone number on your website, that would be a great thing. However, many customers will view your website from their smartphone; it's just a fact of life. And most smartphone users are adept at seeing a telephone number on a website and selecting it on their screen. The smartphone then will dial the number; you will want your customers to do this! However, if you've got the number spelled out as in "555-TECH," the smartphone will not recognize this as a telephone number and you'll be requiring the customers to figure it out for themselves. This is a bad thing.

I suggest rather than a fancy "named" telephone number, consider a toll-free telephone number. In years past, the toll-free number was somewhat of a hassle to deal with but today's technology makes it easy to get and easy to pay for. The issue with a toll-free telephone number is that it's only toll-free for your customers to call you. It's not toll-free for you! You will pay for the minutes your customers use calling into your location, but that can make all the difference to a customer when viewing your company as a whole. It looks professional and legitimate with the best part being that it will get you more customers.

from your computer, from a special VoIP phone, or even from a traditional phone with the correct adapter. You can even use VoIP wirelessly from any spot with wireless connection! Imagine sipping a cup of coffee at a Starbucks while taking business calls.

The equipment you need for VoIP is pretty basic. You will need a high-speed, or broadband, Internet connection—the whole idea is that you are using your Internet connection to make phone calls, right? If you use a traditional phone, you will need a VoIP adapter, which starts at about $35. If you'd rather stick to using the computer exclusively, all you need is the correct software and a microphone; the microphones can be purchased from a place like Best Buy or Walmart for as little as $5.

VoIP has many helpful advanced features. One of the great features of VoIP is the "auto-attendant," which allows you to play special music or prerecorded messages to customers on hold. In addition, an auto-attendant can give customers several choices for directing their call: sales department, billing department, customer service, and so on. It is, in essence, an efficient call-management system that can direct callers wherever you choose.

Even if your business is not yet big enough for auto-attendant to make a huge impact, VoIP's other services are also quite helpful. A feature called "Find Me, Follow Me" (FMFM) allows employees to take business calls that come to the office from outside of the office. For example, when you're out driving, a call to the office can be rerouted directly to your cell phone. FMFM can even be programmed to route calls to certain business lines first before directing them to a cell phone.

The third huge feature of VoIP is "Presence," which is similar to FMFM. You can set the Presence feature to track users, rather than guessing locations as FMFM does. For example, logging into your e-mail from an outside computer will alert Presence to your location, letting it know exactly where you are. You can also set Presence to make sure you do not get calls in specific locations—like your meeting room.

VoIP also includes conferencing capabilities. Audio conferences can be held between multiple people at various distances. You can speak to Joe in Montana and Mary in Wisconsin while holding a meeting at your office in Alabama. Video conferencing is sometimes available through VoIP as well. Files can be exchanged between you, Joe, and Mary using VoIP: Mary can show you the presentation she prepared, Joe can display a chart with your financial statement on it, and you can pull up the schedule for the next meeting.

A final feature to note is the convergence of different technologies using VoIP. Several applications can be run using the same system, with all of the applications aware of everything going on within the system. You can avoid missing an important e-mail by setting the instant messaging system to notify you that you have received a message.

Take some time and look into a VoIP system that might work well for your business, as I am sure that there is an option that will fit your budget. Single lines with toll-free numbers included are less that $70 per month and can make or break the sale when it comes to customer convenience and giving the appearance that you are a legitimate business.

Software

Your home-based computer repair business is cutting edge and modern, simply by virtue of the fact that you'll be working on computers or electronics of some type, depending on your niche. Being surrounded by all of your customer devices, you'll be immersed in a world of keyboards, power supplies, motherboards, and memory. In fact, you'll run your entire business off a computer, for example the desktop or laptop that will be a part of the business's capital assets.

On that computer, you'll be running software that will help you organize and maintain all of the records that you'll need to keep your business on track. To keep that data organized or even create that data, you're going to need a software bundle that you'll use on a daily basis. Now, there is a lot of "pirated" software out there, and just because your friend has a copy that you can "borrow" doesn't mean that you should take it. Since your business is legal and trustworthy, you're going to want to own the licenses for your software purchases, which come with the software, when you purchase it new. Keep your business out of trouble and do yourself a favor . . . buy new software when you need it.

First, let's consider the backbone of the business—the business checking account. It needs to be kept current, balanced, and have you in the know at all times. Yes, you can simply look at your checking account balance on a daily basis to see how much money is there, and you should do so. However, that's not how account records or books are kept and you'll never have an accurate snapshot of your cash position simply by looking at your checking account.

There are some fantastic account software packages out there to help keep you straight. Sage 50 Complete Accounting, QuickBooks Pro, Bookkeeper, AccountEdge, CYMA, and others are readily available on the Internet for purchase or in your local big-box electronics store. Consult your accounting representative or CPA if you're looking for any advice on which accounting software package to purchase, because if you and your CPA have compatible software, it will make tax time a whole lot easier in the future. I personally use QuickBooks Pro on my Mac for account purposes.

Your accounting software is where you can view your profits (or losses), your cash position, your outstanding checks, and everything else financial about your business. Keep in mind that some accounting software programs (like QuickBooks Pro) allow you to run payroll functions, and if you're planning on hiring employees in the future, it's a good time to buy the right account software up front to help you do so.

Microsoft makes a wonderful bundle called Microsoft Office that should be purchased and is available for Windows or Mac operating systems. This software bundle typically comes with Microsoft Word, Microsoft Excel, and Microsoft PowerPoint. Each program serves a different purpose, is compatible with other programs in the suite, and is one of the most common forms of software known today.

- Microsoft Word is a word processor that is basically the main program in the Office suite. When you create a Word document, its extension will be .doc or .docx, which are considered to be the industry standard format of word-processing documents.
- Microsoft Excel is a spreadsheet program that will allow a user to create spreadsheets with intricate formulas to give calculated results. It's also an easy way to collate and organize data, such as price lists and customer account lists, and it's easy to organize these long lists and find necessary data.
- Microsoft PowerPoint is a presentation program that will allow a user to create professional-looking slide shows and presentations, which will come in handy when presenting to a new client.

Now let's hit the Adobe storefront. You're going to need a copy of Adobe Acrobat. A free download from the Adobe website, it's a program that allows you to create, manipulate, print, and manage files in the portable document format (otherwise known as PDF files). This will be important because PDF files, when created by the owner and sent out to others, are for view only and cannot be modified. This will come in handy when e-mailing sensitive documents or contracts.

Since you're most likely going to be creating and implementing your own website, you're going to need a copy of Adobe Photoshop as well. The latest version of Photoshop will allow you to create, develop, save, and use your very own graphics.

Just like copies of software, you want your graphics to be your own creation. Why will you need graphics? No one will buy anything from your website without them. Your website will be a combination of text and graphics to appeal to your customers in the simplest way possible. When I started my first business, I didn't know a thing about Photoshop. I asked a friend for some advice and when I was able to do so, I hired my first graphics designer to help in this department. I had the software, so I put my new graphics designer to good use. My website never looked so good.

Whether you're using a Mac or a PC, you'll find that there are built-in applications that will also be necessary. You will certainly need to use the Internet, so you'll be using your web browser software constantly. You'll need e-mail, so your e-mail program should get a shortcut right to your desktop. You'll also need a calculator. I use the free calculator program that came with my Mac. It's amazing how often I call on my calculator to work up a number or a price quote or help me with a simple math problem when my brain is fried after a long day.

Each business will need its own software programs, and if you plan on starting and hosting your own website, you may need a whole suite of other programs to do so. There are other options here, such as having your website hosted "offsite," and in many cases all you will need is your website browser to manipulate and program changes or new pages, which we will talk about later in this book. Try not to be overcome with software purchases in the beginning—keep it simple if you can.

Tools of the Trade

The tools of the electronics technician are as important as the knowledge he possesses. Without tools, there would be no repairs. With no repairs, there would be no business. While it's going to be difficult to explain all of the tools that are needed for every type of repair on every type of device, we can talk in some generalities.

Good tools are good, but great tools make all the difference. You want professional quality tools. There are lines of tools that are specific to the industry, for example Wiha tools, which offer a 100 percent lifetime satisfaction guarantee. They provide a warranty against defects in workmanship and materials and will replace tools that fail under normal use, forever. You can find these tools at distributors online like kctool.com and others. What makes these tools worth the price? They are high quality, German-made pieces that don't damage customer screws and can "grip" screw heads, torx screws, and other types of screws well. Additionally, they are comfortable to work with. The handles are easy to hold and the tools are light.

Who cares about comfort and weight? You will. Hopefully you'll get an onslaught of business and repair orders will be stacked up. When this happens, if you have a cheap set of "jewelers screwdrivers" that are chewed up and hard to work with, you'll want to throw in the towel. Order the right tools up front, fall in love with a brand, and become a loyal customer.

A simple computer repair technician's tool kit will consist of the following:

1. Precision slotted and Phillips screwdrivers, size 00, 0, 1, and 2
2. A screwdriver magnetizer/demagnetizer
3. Precision nut drivers, size 9/64, 5/32, 3/16, 7/32, 1/4, 5/16, 11/32, 3/8, and 7/16
4. Precision nut drivers, size 5 mm, 5.5 mm, 6 mm, 7 mm, 8 mm, 9 mm, 10 mm, and 11 mm
5. A heat gun (for stripping paint)
6. Compressed air in a can
7. An ESD mat and wrist strap
8. Non-marking pry tools in various sizes
9. Windex and microfiber towels
10. Any specialty tools that are needed per repair

Specialty tools can be defined as "device-specific" tools that have a special purpose. For example, to repair an iPhone 3GS glass panel, you will need a 1.5" suction cup to remove the broken glass panel.

I suggest after you decide what specific line of devices (or maybe all of them!) you choose to work on, you do a little research on the Internet to find out exactly what tools you will need and when. Unlike the inventory I mentioned earlier, it's best to have your tools now, rather than later. Take a long look at the items you want and the items you need, and make your tool purchase appropriately. Learn from my mistakes as a computer repair technician for many years and don't try to use the wrong tool for the wrong job. You'll end up doing more harm than good, which will cost you more in the long run as you're repairing your mistakes.

Tool Checklist

- [ ] Precision slotted and Phillips screwdrivers
  - [ ] Size 00
  - [ ] Size 0
  - [ ] Size 1
  - [ ] Size 2
- [ ] A screwdriver magnetizer/demagnetizer
- [ ] Precision nut drivers
  - [ ] Size 9/64
  - [ ] Size 5/32
  - [ ] Size 3/16
  - [ ] Size 7/32
  - [ ] Size 1/4
  - [ ] Size 5/16
  - [ ] Size 11/32
  - [ ] Size 3/8
  - [ ] Size 7/16
- [ ] Precision nut drivers
  - [ ] Size 5 mm
  - [ ] Size 5.5 mm
  - [ ] Size 6 mm
  - [ ] Size 7 mm
  - [ ] Size 8 mm
  - [ ] Size 9 mm
  - [ ] Size 10 mm
  - [ ] Size 11 mm

- [ ] A heat gun
- [ ] Compressed air in a can
- [ ] ESD mat
- [ ] ESD wrist strap
- [ ] Non-marking pry tools in various sizes
- [ ] Windex
- [ ] Microfiber towels
- [ ] Any specialty tools that are needed per repair

_____

_____

_____

_____

_____

_____

_____

_____

_____

Workstation Organization

Your workstation is the most important area of the workplace because it is where all of your repairs will be done. In order to be able to work effectively, you must keep your workstation organized, clean, and well stocked.

Organization is essential to being able to work effectively. There is no "right" way to organize your workstation as long as you do keep it organized in some manner. Decide on predetermined areas for keeping each tool, part, or what have you.

- Make sure you don't have anything in the area that you don't need. If you don't need that tool right now, put it aside or away.
- Keep anything you need in the area but don't need to work on out of the way. For example, if you have your laptop sitting on your work desk to access order information, make sure the AC adapter is not in the way of your work. Put it behind the desk so that it sits nicely out of sight.
- Keep the tools you use most often close to you. Each repair requires different tools, but if you find yourself doing one kind of repair most often, keep those tools closest to you.

Keeping an organized work area will increase your production rate and make working easier. Work smarter, not harder!

Another way to improve your workstation is by keeping it clean. If you make a mess, don't wait to clean it up. Solving problems as they happen is less stressful in the long run than waiting until several problems pile up. Don't keep anything potentially hazardous near your workstation. Keep all unnecessary items tucked away so that they are not in the way of your work.

Make sure that you always have everything you need on hand. Work ahead, ordering inventory and stocking parts you need as you notice you are getting low. If you wait until you are out of what you need, your production will be slowed, maybe even halted until you get a chance to place a stocking order. Make a list of everything you need and find a way to notify yourself if you are getting close to running out of anything.

04 | Writing a Business Plan

Business plan, management plan, financial plan . . . aggh! I know, you are thinking that now may be the perfect time to jump ship. Give yourself a bit more credit; you can do this. With a little research and planning, creating these necessary documents can be easy and empowering. Nothing says "I am my own boss, I own my own business!" more than creating and advertising your mission, objectives, personal plan, and cash-flow objectives!

I've mentioned organization before, and this is yet another example of how important organization and documentation are to starting and securing your own home-based business. Start out by listing each of the headings that are essential to creating these all-important plans. Put the already-established vision of your business in the forefront of your mind and create the guiding policies and procedures that will define your business and set you apart from the competition.

Remember that supportive family and those trusted advisers? Meet with those individuals and talk through your plans. Bounce ideas off of these people and get their advice. This is your business so only consider the suggestions that match your end goals. Remember the evolution we have talked about and are hoping for? These plans are the heart of the early stages of your business, but they may change with your growth. That is OK, too. Don't feel bound, but don't lack the focus and effort that this step requires. In fact some of these documents will be necessary, not optional, so get to it.

Now, pick up your pencil and notepad and get started. Create the home-based business that you've always dreamed of owning . . . the one that balances your life and fuels your passion!

Why a Business Plan Is Important

A business plan helps you keep your thoughts straight and acts as a guideline as you progress down the path to opening day. As you approach a bank for financing, it will be required. It also helps you validate the concept of the business and sets clear goals. For our example, the business name will be NEWCO, LLC being opened in ANYTOWN, USA, and is owned by the very successful Mr. John Doe. In this chapter, you'll see a complete sample business plan laid out as it would be presented to a bank.

As usual, you should have all of your documents reviewed by your lawyer as you progress through your business start-up, for advice on other issues, laws, and thoughts that might not be listed here.

Cover Sheet

The cover sheet of your business plan should simply include the name of business, name of principal (you), address, and telephone number of business.

NEWCO, LLC
Mr. John Doe
ANYTOWN, USA
(555) 555-5555

Table of Contents

Here is a sample of a typical Table of Contents (each entry would be followed by the corresponding page number).

Executive Summary & Statement of Purpose

Electronic devices have revolutionized the communications arena, redefining how we run our lives. Cellular phones, computers, tablets, and MP3 players are in high demand and remain costly consumer products. As a result, high-quality, affordable services and repairs are in high demand. There is a fair amount of competition in the market, but a new business can easily stand out by being a trusted and honest repair center. The electronics repair industry is a multibillion-dollar industry, and a good game plan can set a new business apart from the rest.

Today, cellular phones and other handheld devices are truly consumer electronic devices with an estimated 300 million customers and growing. Cell phones and tablets have ceased to be an exclusive status symbol of high-powered lawyers and are now in the hands of millions of consumers from elementary school age to the elderly.

NEWCO, LLC is taking advantage of an opportunity to become a highly distinguished and recognized leader in the electronics repair industry. It is the goal of our company to become established as the leading electronics service provider for the metro ANYTOWN area.

In order to achieve this goal, NEWCO's critical success factors will be to identify emerging trends and integrate them into our company operations, respond quickly to and anticipate technology changes, provide high-quality services, invest time and money in marketing and advertising, expand into specialty markets, and stay up-to-date with the "technology curve."

The company is initially formed as a Limited Liability Company in ANYTOWN, and will succeed tremendously in this market. Capitalizing on the growing wireless communications industry and based on their success in ANYTOWN, a decision to expand company operations across the US and create a niche market for its services, products, and accessories is planned for the near future.

Keys to Success

Our company keys to success will include:

1. Provide excellent customer service
2. Grow and maintain a referral network of customers.
3. Focus expertise on servicing of tablets, smartphones, and computers.
4. Respond rapidly to customer problems with service or a plan.

Mission

NEWCO's mission is to offer its customers the highest quality repair services and products. Its owner focuses on personalized service to his customers by offering convenience and rapid, reliable service. Additionally, NEWCO has the technological expertise to assist customers in picking a service that best meets their needs. Finally, our staff will have strong vendor relationships with product suppliers and will be able to meet customers' demand for repairs of even the newest technology.

We believe it is important to remain an active member of the community and to impact people's lives in more ways than deriving a profit from them. We propose to host community events and belong to our local chamber of commerce to bring out the best in people.

Objectives

The company plans to focus on the following target markets that will provide us with the greatest market penetration: specialty business users, general business users, and personal users. We intend to offer service packages that are priced appropriately for each segment and will offer the repairs that best suit each segment's needs.

The Metro ANYTOWN area is populated today by more than 700,000 inhabitants and is home to ten Fortune 500 and fourteen Fortune 1,000 company headquarters. The Metropolitan ANYTOWN Chamber of Commerce and corporate executives are committed to actively recruiting new companies to the region. Public and private partnerships with business, financial, and nonprofit communities are key to spurring quality job creation and investment throughout the city's neighborhoods.

Our company will center on serving the ANYTOWN community (which is currently growing at a rate of 6 percent per year) as well as concentrating on the local population, banking on the growing trend of using mobile phones and other hand-held electronic devices.

Business Objectives

- Achieve company growth.
- Become established as the leading repair center for smartphones, tablets, and laptop computers.
- Increase number of dealer and school customers.

Financial Objectives

- Create and increase revenue.

Marketing Objectives

- Increase marketing efforts.
- Expand market area.
- Expand marketing reach.
- Establish brand recognition.

Company Description

Electronics service and repair company offering repair packages to end users and corporate accounts alike.

Company Summary

NEWCO, LLC will offer its customers first-class electronic services with twenty-four-hour turnaround service at excellent prices.

Market demand drives electronics manufacturers and distributors to offer new and improved products to the market. The demand for newer technology with more visual interaction and entertainment is great, and families in the United States are spending a tremendous amount of their income on said devices. Smartphones have definitely become an important part of people's lives all over the world. The average phone in the US may be purchased under a subsidized plan through a cell-phone carrier, with a prohibitively expensive repair option.

We believe that, with our solid plan and thorough knowledge of the electronics repair industry, our company will be in the perfect location to start our operations in the US, and it will start operating in the right time. NEWCO, LLC will provide its customers support and convenience second to none.

Company Ownership

NEWCO, LLC is wholly owned by Mr. John Doe, residing in ANYTOWN, USA.

Start-up Summary

Mr. Doe will invest $10,000 in NEWCO, LLC. He will also invest an additional $5,000 when operation takes off in March Year 1.

Services & Products

The following are the services that will be offered by NEWCO, LLC:

- Smartphone repairs: Apple, HTC, Samsung, Motorola, and others
- Tablet repairs: Apple, Asus, and Kindle
- Laptop computer repairs: Apple, Dell, and HP

Marketing Plan

The market potential is huge for our services, evidenced by what appears to be the unstoppable growth of the handheld electronics industry. Currently, the telecom industry is among the strongest growth industries and is responsible for huge gains in the capital markets. The proliferation of cellular phones is increasing at rates that at one time were unimaginable. One illustrative example is that it is forecast that within two years over 65 percent of children from age of ten to fifteen will have cell phones.

Future growth of the market/products is projected in the following areas:

- Smartphones. With the advent of text messaging, users can send regular short-message service (SMS) or e-mail on their phones. This leads to an unprecedented use of smartphones at an almost epidemic level. Nevertheless, the more advanced these devices become, the more fragile they are. The touch screen on almost all new smartphone devices is made of glass. One drop and it will crack.
- Tablets. At first glance, many customers may think that tablets are overrated, large-scale handheld devices. However, the trend to use tablets is quickly growing—growing so fast that tablet sales may even overtake the sales of laptop computers sometime in the near future. Once again, handheld devices such as tablets are designed to be just that—held in the hand. Humans have a natural tendency to make mistakes, which can lead to dropping devices or otherwise damaging them.

Our company will try to take advantage of these developments and serve the best interests of its customers while keeping handheld devices from entering landfills prematurely.

Market Segmentation

NEWCO, LLC will focus on five customer groups, bearing in mind that it is quite customary today to have more than one cell phone, tablet, and computer per family:

- Children in the age group of ten to seventeen years old
- College students
- Adult general public
- Professionals
- Service organizations and companies that are responsible for large-scale electronics programs

Competition & Buying Patterns

Brand names are of high importance, and the key to consumer buying decisions is the marketing tactics they are exposed to. As has been pointed out, there are other sellers with services similar to those supplied by NEWCO, LLC, and they may even be less expensive. It is essential to realize that we will build brand reputation and run an honest business. Most importantly, our services must ultimately be available on a nationwide level to reach this expansive market.

The need to attract, acquire, leverage, and retain customers remains a primary concern of business. Revenue growth through customer acquisition and retention is as important a requirement in e-commerce as it is in other businesses. Customers count speed of service as a key reason they do business with a company. They resent delays and hate waiting for service. In the United States, almost 80 percent of the gross domestic product (GDP) is generated through different kinds of services, and a company that distinguishes itself with quality work while offering expedited lead times will impress customers. Customers generally are not thrilled if they receive good service, but they are highly dissatisfied if they do not. NEWCO, LLC will provide the necessary framework to cope with these demands by cutting the waiting time for service.

Customers also want consistent, reliable, and easy-to-use service. As the speed of service increases, customer expectations grow, making friendly, easy, and solution-oriented customer service an important business trend.

Soon, shoppers will simply wave their cell phone over the item they want and the charge will automatically appear on their cell-phone bill. It's happening in some cities overseas already. And right now, MasterCard and Motorola are testing a similar program here in the United States. Retailers have registers that will take the signal from the cell phone, and the purchase is automatically converted to a MasterCard charge. Buyers don't have to sign anything. There is concern that if this feature stopped working and was in need of service, it would be like losing your wallet. Speed and trustworthiness will be paramount.

NEWCO, LLC is planning to take advantage of these trends in technology. We shall also be very quick in establishing our own website to take advantage of e-trade.

Operations

The operations of NEWCO, LLC will be maintained at a residential office location until such time that finances permit the lease of a commercial location within the city of Anytown, USA.

Proper equipment, technician stations, tools, and lighting will be present.

Each service performed will include a thorough quality-control check prior to delivery to ensure complete and correct repair.

Management Plan

The management of NEWCO, LLC is made up of the owner, who will provide the marketing, operations, and service for the business.

Personnel Plan

The NEWCO online store will operate virtually twenty-four hours a day, seven days a week. Although the store opening hours will officially be 10:00 a.m. to 5:00 p.m., it is clear that with our Internet operation, customer support will be available nonstop. The personnel plan will be developed and refined as customer support increases.

Assumptions regarding personnel have been made for year 1 through year 3 as follows:

- Year 1 ending March 2013—Owner, Mr. John Doe, will draw a salary of $40,000.
- Year 2 ending March 2014—Salaries will be boosted by 10 to 15 percent. Additional staff will be hired if significant increases in sales warrant.
- The same applies to Year 3 ending March 2015.

Personal Balance Sheet

It is assumed that the owner's private resources will be sufficient to finance any monthly cash-flow shortage. However, it would be advisable to establish a bank relationship as soon as possible. Sales could very well increase at a much sharper rate than assumed in initial conservative projections. Sharper sales will result in a greater need for funds in support of inventory and receivables. An overdraft line of credit with the bank will be an excellent cushion to fall back on.

A shorter learning curve will be brought to the business by the owner due to his extensive background and in-depth market knowledge. He has a clear understanding of the need to manage costs and forecast future needs so that the business is not "broadsided" by the unexpected.

One other component on which the financial plan is based is wise purchases. Finding the right product at the right price will enable the business to meet planned margins and maintain inventory at an attractive level with a high turn rate.

Start-Up Funding

Mr. John Doe will invest $10,000 in NEWCO, LLC to cover start-up costs. He will also invest an additional $5,000 when operation takes off in March 2013. The cash-flow projection available shortly will show the necessity and use of the funds.

Important Assumptions

As a general rule the company will not sell on credit. However, for very special cases we might offer short-term credit against valid assurances. We shall accept cash and checks, Visa, MasterCard, Discover, and American Express, and PayPal on the Internet. All sales paid via credit cards will be deposited in our business checking account within forty-eight hours.

Financial Plan

Our financial plan charts the course for our new business and is ever evolving as we start up. It's an ongoing and living document. This is a conservative view of our plans and expectations in the market and within ourselves. We don't have a "hockey stick" forecast, one that predicts skyrocketing sales figures that in chart form look like a hockey stick. Rather, we have carefully studied and analyzed the market and believe that our financial plan is accurate and correctly represents our new venture.

Start-Up Expenses

The start-up expenses for the business are greatly reduced, compared to other businesses. The company owner will maintain an office and toll-free telephone line at his residence. This gives our business an immediate advantage over other traditional start-ups and offers a low barrier to entry.

With this advantage, NEWCO, LLC strives to remain lean and aggressive and to utilize many capital assets that are already owned. Therefore, the worksheet on page 69 summarizes the start-up expenses and expenditures that will be purchased at or just before business launch.

Cash-Flow Projection

Our cash-flow projection outlines our cash position, month to month, starting in January with the $10,000 injection and assuming modest sales ramp up over a twelve-month period. (Note from author: See an example of this on page 114). This cash-flow projection shows how beginning in April of the first year, the cash position of the business improves each month, simultaneously allowing wages to be paid and increased.

In month seven (July), we plan on hiring our first full-time employee, which will give us the opportunity to grow the business and stay on plan.

NEWCO, LLC Start-up Expenses Worksheet

EXPENSE	CASH BUDGETED
Accounting Services	$100.00
Advertising	$250.00
Cash	$100.00
Equipment - CPU	$829.00
Equipment - Tools	$190.00
Equipment - Bench	$520.00
Insurance	$139.00
Internet Service	$62.00
Legal Costs	$100.00
Office Supplies	$300.00
Rent	$1,215.00
Software	$500.00
Starting Inventory	$1,830.00
Telephone Service	$88.00
Website Service	$99.00
Total Start-up Costs	**$6,322.00**

Balance Sheet

Our balance sheet summarizes our company assets, liabilities, and equity a month after start-up. The business will implement its marketing plan in the second month of operations, steadily increasing the advertising budget to grow sales. We will provide an accurate balance sheet over the course of business as it develops.

Appendices

Note from author: The information within the appendix is highly confidential. As a result, provide the information only on a discretionary basis.

If you have provided complete and accurate materials within your business plan, you will have several supporting documents that will be represented here. Ideas that might be included in your business plan appendix are marketing materials that you have created, your business logo, and copies of your business cards if you have them.

Most of your business's supporting information can be included within the body of the business plan. Reserve the appendix for information that supports the business financials, including tax returns, inventory estimates, and personal and business credit-history information. Also use it for any general supporting documents that are longer than two pages, along with formal contracts, supporting pictures, and market-research information. Market research or studies help a great deal when you present your business plan to an investor, so be sure to include those as well.

Essentially, the appendices of your business plan will be referred to as necessary and should be simple, clean, and organized according to each section of the business plan. Organize and label the documents according to the reference order within the business plan. Always include clear, legible copies. Never include the original documents. Visit sba.gov for templates.

With all of the pieces of the puzzle coming together in your plan, it's time to start making your dreams of being a business owner become a reality. In today's Internet world just about every man, woman, and school-aged child is connected to the web via smartphone or computer. You need to build a website.

Getting a website up and live will present to the world a technologically astute business that has a storefront, at least on the Internet. Again, this is Business 101 in this century and you will find that your website will quickly become one of the most valuable pieces of your business.

At this stage of the game you're going to want to secure your funding, and it's a great time to approach your bank if you need to borrow some money or ask for special financing. Knowing how much business capital you have at the outset is going to be a very important step of the process.

Additionally, once you start taking orders and bringing customer units into your location, you are going to want to have a business insurance policy in place. Get this going as soon as you anticipate your first sale. There is liability that comes with receiving a customer at your office and then being responsible for the expensive electronic device left with you. In business you should make sure to err on the side of caution, and a typical business liability insurance policy is quite affordable.

Building Your Website

Think of your website as a necessary facet of your business. Whether you create it yourself or whether you use an outside source to complete your website, this process will take time and capital. Most importantly, the text and "body" of the website will need to be custom written and this will most certainly come from you, the business owner, as there is no one more closely aware of the way your business needs to be portrayed to the public.

By now you have your domain name (which will be the name of the site as found on the Internet), your business name (as registered with the IRS), and your logo (graphic branding), so you are ready to get started with the building and release of your website—aka online store.

Building websites is a topic in itself, with many books and publications written on the subject. We cannot take the plunge into how to create a website from scratch, so we will proceed under the assumption that you have basic website knowledge, you will use an e-commerce solution, or you will hire a service to get things going for you. If you do hire this process out to a separate firm, make sure that you will have the ability to make changes, add new services, and otherwise update the website at your location. Also get in writing that you are the sole owner of the site and have full rights to your website data after the initial setup is completed. Don't get caught in a contract that requires you to spend a bucket full of money just to change the business hours on your "About Us" page unless that's what you're looking for!

All websites must take into consideration several factors. Designing an effective website requires more than just facts on a page, then uploading it to the web. In fact, in this industry I would bet that your website will be just as effective as your telephone number when it comes to making sales. It's a silent salesperson that conveys information—important information—to your prospective clients before they even have a chance to talk to you. For this simple reason, you are going to want a well-thought-out website that gives you the upper hand when customers are shopping for a firm to use when they need a computer repair. You should strive above all to be clean and engaging in every aspect of the website design, or you may quickly lose your audience.

Before you begin, consider your audience: customers who are in need of computer repair. Then put yourself into their shoes. Perform an Internet search as if you were a customer, then read the results that come up. While you're doing this, get out your notepad and start taking notes on things that you like, what some of the competition is doing to make a sale, and overall design cues that appeal to you. Truthfully, the design of your site needs to appeal to you too, since you will be staring at it, well, for the entire time you are in business!

Websites are somewhat like a family tree. Use your notepad to draw out what you might like this tree to look like. Start at the bottom of your paper and draw a square (to represent a single page on your website) and write "Home Page" in it. This is where your tree will start. Every website has a home page, also known as the first page. This is the page that will pop up when you type your domain name into a search bar on the Internet, so of course this page needs to be amazing!

The home page is the roots and trunk of your tree. Next draw a short line upward (to represent the branch, or "link," on your website) connecting to another square (page). What should you put in this square? "About Us."

Your "About Us" is a critical component within your website that many customers will use. Look at other website About Us pages. They list hours of operation, addresses, contact information, and most will have a brief description of what the company provides and some even have employee biographies to give the business a "human" feel.

Next, let's draw a branch and another square coming off the Home Page that says "Services." From there draw a branch that says "Desktop Computers" and a separate branch that says "Laptop Computers." You can continue growing your tree with whatever pertinent information you think will be a part of your site.

What you're doing is creating a plan to build a website. This website tree that you're making will help you move forward, whether you ultimately create and publish your own website or use a consultant to do it for you.

As you make progress on your website tree, you'll find that the tree branches stop. This means that there are no links leaving that page, only a link to the page. This is OK, but for search engines to properly scan your website to rank your relevancy on the Internet, you may consider branching (linking) pages together so there are no "dead ends." You want to optimize your site with a nice, consistent flow so that it's organized with one page linking to another to give your site depth.

Site Layout

Strive for consistency. You want your website to have an identity, preferably with your newly designed business logo at the top, which should remain at the top of every page to give a uniform feel. This also indicates that you're still on your website when clicking links from one page to the next. It's frustrating to me if I feel "lost" on a website or if I am diverted to another site. I'll end up gravitating to a different site that appeals to me.

To help your customers with navigation, you are going to provide a rich set of links within your site. Ideally there will be multiple ways for your customers to navigate your pages. Consider including a link near the top that says "HOME," so the customer can always got back to the beginning of your site and get to your home page—from any page. Additionally, a navigation section that is also consistent on every page will allow customers to quickly move to different sections on your site. In webmaster language, if this navigation section is across the top of your site, it's called the "navtop." If the navigation is down the left side of your page, it's called the "navleft." Now you're starting to think like a true web professional!

Your navtop or navleft will contain useful and pertinent links to pages that will quickly help customers get the information they are looking for. Whether it's your "About Us" page or your "Services" page, if it takes too long for customers to find what they need, they will leave your site and visit a competitor's site that works better for them. Too many clicks to retrieve information results in lost sales.

Also, as you're thinking about your website design, graphics will play an important role in achieving your website goals. Have you ever been at a restaurant looking over a menu, and eyeballed the pictures of an entree, rather than reading all of the available options? I've been known to point at a picture on a menu when the server asks, "What would you like?" All I have to say is, "I want this."

The same will hold true with your site. The pictures (graphics) that you design and use will appeal to many of your users, and quite frankly if your site visitors are picture lovers like me, you can sell your services without any words. How amazing is that? Make a sale without words.

Conversely, you'll never want your customer to land on one of your pages that is made up entirely of text for the very opposite reason. It's not appealing and frankly with the number of opinions that are rolling around in their mind about your business before they become a customer, you don't want them to have to work for it.

So while thinking about your layout, keep in mind that the top left corner is the most important part of any page, just like a school report or business document. We are taught to read from left to right, top to bottom. This means that your logo and business name should be at the top left, and remain at the top left, on every page.

The Web Medium

Once you have a good layout in mind and once the HTML code starts developing, you'll want to provide opportunities for your customers to interact with your business. Add "e-mail us" links. Add a "log in to my account" section. Install a "sign up for our newsletter" application that gathers your customers' e-mail addresses and stores them for e-mail marketing.

The web medium is different from print because you can interact with your customers in this way. However, don't mistake a clean, elegant website design for pizzazz. Just because you can make an animated jpeg with a dancing computer that also flies across the screen doesn't mean that you should do it. Elegance and simplicity work much better. Too many flashing lights, colors, drop-down boxes, and graphics will strain your customer's eyes. Likewise it's best to avoid automatically playing any MP3 files, or sound files, that might annoy or distract a customer upon visiting your website. Bear in mind that for some people computer time is quiet time. You don't want to raise your customers' heart rate, hence raise their blood pressure and drive them away. Underwhelm them with a clean and simple design rather than overwhelm them with gimmicks.

Your Message

Your website is your silent salesperson, your billboard and storefront, and face of the business. You need to give your potential customers a reason to stay on the site and give them an answer to the question "what can I get out of being here?"

This doesn't mean that you need to give away a free computer for visiting or movie tickets for clicking the Facebook "Like" button. What you should give your customers is information, advice, help with a problem, opportunities to solve a dilemma, or a link to a useful page. This is what your business is going to be designed for. It's why you're starting your computer repair business. You are providing a solution to customers who have a problem, and all you need to do is convince them that you are the best place to provide that solution. Make it easy for your customers to follow links to pinpoint their specific needed repair, then offer a competitive price and you'll make a sale.

Graphics & Colors

You should know that speed is the key to keeping visitors on your site. Your potential customers will get impatient if it takes too long for pages to load, so keep the sizes of your graphics in mind when they are being created, ideally keeping each graphic under 6k to 8k bytes.

Graphics are an extremely important part of your site, so you will want to create original graphics for your original site. Never copy graphics from another site—not only is it a copyright infringement, it is in bad taste. Anyone can steal someone else's hard work; it's up to you to come up with original work that will keep your customers excited to see what's behind the next link!

Graphics can also quickly tell the story on a page. You can help your site's "skim-mability" by placing graphics in strategic locations with small blurbs of text to keep readers focused on your goal—to complete an order. Since your site is going to be all about computer repair, then you should have a picture of a broken device, a picture of yourself repairing a device, and a picture of a repaired device. This "story" is easy to "read" and it makes sense on your site. Including a "how it works" storyboard is very appealing and helps ease the customer into trusting your brand. At least you can show that you are human, you really work on computers, and you have some experience. A picture is worth a thousand words. And in this case, you can make a sale without words. Once again, this is an amazing concept!

Additionally, colors are important to the success of your site. Red and orange excite the senses and increase the heart rate. Green and blue are very restful. Yellow reminds people of sunshine and is a "happy" color. Consider the use of colors on your site to keep the effects of your presentation positive.

You May Need to Experiment

I tried an experiment after I got my website up, running, and taking orders. Yes, it was working, and I could view the analytics of the site and see the thousands of customers visiting the site, but then leaving and not ordering. "What happened? How can I convert the visits to sales?" So I started looking over my website. I had a light green background with white pages, a pleasant-looking site, but maybe it wasn't appealing to everyone.

So I made a mirror of the site, kept the same prices, most of the same text, and changed the colors of the background to black, and a lot of my white colors to red. At first look I was pleased with my black-and-red website and I was excited to see how many more orders I would take with it.

So I uploaded the new template and went live.

To my surprise, my sales nearly stopped. I was in a complete panic, and my site was driving people away. I was shocked to learn that a simple color swap was so distracting to my visitors that they quickly clicked away, never to return.

Lesson learned; you will always have people visiting your website and they will not all buy from you, but don't help them leave. Help them stay and start by picking your site colors wisely.

Color decisions also apply to the color of the text that is on each page. A typical page is white with black text. If you have a black page, black text won't work so you would choose white or another color. Red text alerts or "warns" the reader to "look here." Green text on a light green page is somewhat camouflaged. Try different text colors and you'll see for yourself what works and what doesn't.

Current Information

One of my biggest pet peeves when I visit a website is when I notice that the site is not current. A glaring sign of a neglected website is time-sensitive information that long ago became invalid—for example, a July special on the home page displaying in the month of December. I also have a strange habit of looking at the bottom of websites at the copyright dates. Most current sites have the © Copyright plus "BUSINESS NAME" plus "CURRENT YEAR." When I visit a site and they have a copyright year that's a few years past, I feel that the site is dead and inactive. Therefore, it's not somewhere I want to be.

Take the steps to make sure that your site stays current. Stale sites fall to the bottom of the website rankings and current, eventful, and informative sites rise to the top.

Navigation

All websites must have some sort of navigation to get from one page to the next, unless you have a single-page website.

Single-page websites sound appealing to some, but the amount of information that you're likely going to be adding to your website needs to be organized with a clear path of navigation. Furthermore, single-page websites lack depth, which will also hurt your website rankings within the search engines.

You want a deep, rich, interesting, and informative website that has a home page, with a set of links on the left or top to get to the next page.

Your navigation should never lead to a dead-end unless it's the last page after customers check out online, and even then you should give them a "back to home page" navigation link.

With that being said, navigation is simply links within your site to other pages on your site. Keeping this link tree in order takes a little thought in the beginning, but it will be a necessary step in creating your new website.

Privacy Statement

Your website's privacy statement is a page telling your customers and visitors who spend time on your site what information you collect and what you will do with that information. Simply put, it is a short explanation of what you are doing to observe visitors on your website.

There are a number of sites that will help you create a privacy policy for free, such as www.freeprivacypolicy.com (also see the sample below).

Sample Privacy Statement

What information do we collect?

- We collect information from you when you register on the site, place an order, enter a contest or sweepstakes, respond to a survey or communication such as e-mail, or participate in another site feature.

- When you are ordering or registering, we may ask you for your name, e-mail address, mailing address, phone number, credit-card information, or other information. You may, however, visit our site anonymously.

- We also collect information about gift recipients so that we can fulfill a gift purchase. The information we collect about gift recipients is not used for marketing purposes.

- Like many websites, we use "cookies" to enhance your experience and gather information about visitors and visits to our websites. Please refer to the "Do we use 'cookies'?" section below for information about cookies and how we use them.

How do we use your information?

We may use the information we collect from you when you register, purchase products, enter a contest or promotion, respond to a survey or marketing communication, surf the website, or use certain other site features in the following ways:

- To personalize your site experience and to allow us to deliver the type of content and product offerings in which you are most interested.

- To allow us to better service you and respond to your customer-service requests.

- To quickly process your transactions.

- To administer a contest, promotion, survey, or other site feature.

- If you have opted-in to receive our e-mail newsletter, we may send you periodic e-mails. If you would no longer like to receive promotional e-mail from us, please refer to the "How can you opt-out, remove, or modify information you have provided to us?" section below. If you have not opted-in to receive e-mail newsletters, you will not receive these e-mails. Visitors who register or participate in other site features such as marketing programs and "members-only" content will be given a choice whether they would like to be on our e-mail list and receive e-mail communications from us.

How do we protect visitor information?

We implement a variety of security measures to maintain the safety of your personal information. Your personal information is contained behind secured networks and is accessible only by a limited number of persons who have special access rights to such systems and are required to keep the information confidential. When you place orders or access your personal information, we offer the use of a secure server. All sensitive/credit information you supply is transmitted via Secure Socket Layer (SSL) technology and then encrypted into our databases to be accessed only as stated above.

Do we use "cookies"?

Yes. Cookies are small files that a site or its service provider transfers to your computer's hard drive through your web browser (if you allow) that enables the site's or service provider's systems to recognize your browser and capture and remember certain information. For instance, we use cookies to help us remember and process the items in your shopping cart. They are also used to help us understand your preferences based on previous or current site activity, which enables us to provide you with improved services. We also use cookies to help us compile aggregate data about site traffic and site interaction so that we can offer better site experiences and tools in the future.

We may contract with third-party service providers to assist us in better understanding our site visitors. These service providers are not permitted to use the information collected on our behalf except to help us conduct and improve our business.

You can choose to have your computer warn you each time a cookie is being sent, or you can choose to turn off all cookies. You do this through your browser (like Firefox or Internet Explorer) settings. Each browser is a little different, so look at your browser Help menu to learn the correct way to modify your cookies. If you turn cookies off, you won't have access to many features that make your site experience more efficient and some of our services will not function properly. However, you can still place orders over the telephone by contacting customer service.

Do we disclose the information we collect to outside parties?

We do not sell, trade, or otherwise transfer to outside parties your personally identifiable information unless we provide you with advance notice, except as described below. The term "outside parties" does not include our business. It also does not include website hosting partners and other parties who assist us in operating our website, conducting our business, or serving you, as long as those parties agree to keep this information confidential. We may also release your information when we believe release is appropriate to comply with the law, enforce our site policies, or protect ours or others' rights, property, or safety.

However, non-personally identifiable visitor information may be provided to other parties for marketing, advertising, or other uses.

How can you opt-out or remove or modify information you have provided to us?

To modify your e-mail subscriptions, please let us know by modifying your preferences in the "My Account" section. Please note that due to e-mail production schedules you may receive any e-mails already in production.

To delete all of your online account information from our database, sign into the "My Account" section of our site and remove your shipping addresses, billing addresses and payment information. Please note that we may maintain information about an individual sales transaction in order to service that transaction and for record-keeping.

Third-party links

In an attempt to provide you with increased value, we may include third-party links on our site. These linked sites have separate and independent privacy policies. We therefore have no responsibility or liability for the content and activities of these linked sites. Nonetheless, we seek to protect the integrity of our site and welcome any feedback about these linked sites (including if a specific link does not work).

Changes to our policy

If we decide to change our privacy policy, we will post those changes on this page. Policy changes will apply only to information collected after the date of the change. This policy was last modified on May 1, 2013.

Questions & feedback
We welcome your questions, comments, and concerns about privacy. Please send us any and all feedback pertaining to privacy, or any other issue.

Online policy only
This online privacy policy applies only to information collected through our website and not to information collected offline.

Terms and conditions
Please also visit our Terms and Conditions establishing the use, disclaimers, and limitations of liability governing the use of our website.

Your consent
By using our site, you consent to our privacy policy.

Your site's privacy policy is one of the most important legal parts of your website. It gives your customers a feeling of security and peace of mind. Have a well-written privacy policy available gives the website a professional image. In many cases when you sing up for online marketing, you must have a privacy policy in place and clickable from the home page on your website.

Terms & Conditions
Terms and conditions are most critical as well, and they are designed to keep you and your customer safe and in the know when making a purchase on your website. In the not so distant past, a good many webmasters just copied the terms and conditions word for word from another site that had terms and conditions looking legitimate enough to assume that they were written by a lawyer who knew something about the subject. You need to think about your own Terms and Conditions, including your refund and returns policy and other pertinent conditions that help you run your business.

I am here to tell you that one business's Terms and Conditions page doesn't always work for another. Essentially the Terms and Conditions page is a contract. However, just because you have Terms and Conditions posted on your website doesn't mean they have been accepted. That is the first point you should take from this section.

You can "force" the acceptance of the Terms and Conditions, usually by having your customers click an "I accept" button with a link to the Terms and Conditions page, before they make a purchase from your site. This is called a "click-wrap agreement." Good click-wrap agreements are the ones in which the default setting reads "I do not agree," so the customer must change the selection to the "I agree" button, and then click. The reason is that the customer must consciously make the decision to agree to your terms.

One of the most important components of your Terms and Conditions may have to do with dispute resolution. Let's say you operate a website in Kansas and have a disgruntled customer in California. If the customer in California defrauds your Kansas-based business, you could sue the customer in California, and in fact would be required to utilize the court system of California to collect any money. Turnabout is fair play, and the customer also can sue you in California. However, courts consistently have held that the parties to a contract can agree in advance to the place (venue) where disputes arising from it are resolved, as long as the venue has some interest in the dispute (e.g., one of the parties lives there or the contract is to be performed there). This sometimes is called a "choice of forum" clause, perhaps the most important term or condition—and is the second point you should take from this section.

Another aspect of your conditions involves how (as opposed to where) disputes are resolved. Terms and Conditions can specify that disputes will be resolved by arbitration, and this is the third point. Taking a situation to arbitration may be a better solution for all parties involved, financially speaking, if your Terms and Conditions have provided for this.

The last point that we need to discuss is the possibility of incurring attorney's fees during a lawsuit. Let's face it, you are much more likely than your customers to make a mistake, and it's typical for each party to bear the cost of its own attorney. Add a provision that states that you will not pay for your opponent's attorney fees, to protect yourself from frivolous or negligent lawsuits.

Testimonials

Testimonials are real customers writing positive reviews about your service. Real customer testimonials bring confidence. I have received thousands of customer testimonials from hundreds of thousands of repairs at my business. My point is that customer testimonials require actual handwritten work from your customers and they need to really be impressed to make this effort. Therefore, only a small percentage of your jobs will result in testimonials, which you should hold on to dearly and proudly display for all of your customers to see.

If customers took the time to write to you, you should honor them by displaying their comments on your site. Create a customer testimonial page that shows their praise.

Make a Difference in a Customer's Life

I've been in business for years, and it still surprises me when I have a customer write in with a thank you. I take this as a very personal part of the business and swell with pride when these messages come through. It's easy for people to complain—and it's hard for people to offer praise. One of my favorite customer testimonials that I display proudly in my office is:

Dear Ryan Arter at Mission Repair,

Thank you, thank you, thank you! When I tried to close the canopy of the [jet] and it just would not shut . . . I knew something was wrong. When I climbed up to see what was in the way, it turned out to be my Apple MacBook Pro! Yikes! I love my computer and now it was damaged . . . badly. Let's just say the canopy won!

Not sure whom to turn to or what the prognosis would be, I was told to call Mission Repair, so I did.

Your staff was so professional and timely. I could not be happier with the repair work, and my beloved computer is looking great and working 100 percent! Thank you all so much for your excellent customer service, talented personnel, quick update, and timely turnaround! I would recommend your services to anyone looking! Thanks a ton!

Very respectfully,
Lt. Amy

Words

Now let's talk about the most important part of your site—the language on the site—because if this part is faulty, the rest of your work will be largely wasted. Have you ever been to a site and caught a spelling error? How about careless grammar or punctuation?

Truthfully, since I've written and published several websites myself, I do give some leeway in this regard; however, the general public does not. There are some amazing spellers out there, so if you know you're not the best speller, you must have all your work proofread. Error-ridden text reflects badly on the site owner and it conveys that you're careless, lazy, illiterate, or just plain sloppy. Would you want to have someone with any of those traits work on your computer? No way. Most customers would not entrust any of their hard-earned money to business owners who don't even care enough to check the correctness of their own site.

You can take steps to improve your writing skills, and you can have a friend proofread your work. If all else fails, you can employ someone to write the text for you, but be forewarned that this can be an expensive endeavor and you will be entrusting your ideas and emotions to someone else's text. As the business owner, make it a goal to be the writer; it'll pay off in the long run.

Build a Relationship with Your Bank

This is a tough subject and when I first started my business I constantly heard words like "collateral" and "EBITDA" and "DUNS" that ultimately ended up in "declined" credit requests.

You should consider your banker one of your partners, and if you don't feel this way you should find another one. Here are a few questions to ask yourself to help determine if you are working with a banker who is on your side.

- What is your bank doing to provide value-added services? Does your bank provide educational seminars on topics that will help you do a better job of managing and growing your business?

    Are the products offered by your bank focused on what small businesses need, or do they seem to be designed more for the bank's convenience and success?

    Look for interest-bearing checking and savings accounts, which most banks will certainly provide for free. In fact some banks make small businesses a priority and will incentivize with offers and cash deposits for meeting certain criteria. Free money from a bank is not common but is not unheard of!

- Does your bank offer back-up employees to stand in when your primary contact is away from the bank? Make sure that you personally know each of the responsible employees. I believe that banking in person develops relationships much faster than banking solely online. Since you can't always count on having the bank manager at your fingertips when you need him or her, it's good to get to know the regular staff, remember their names, and ultimately have an entire bank branch on your side.

  You can go one step farther and open an account at another bank as a backup. In the beginning it may be tough to get a large credit line without some business traction, but since you're in for the long haul, when the time is right having a little competition between banks may be the key to your financial freedom.

- Find out if and how your banker is taking your total banking activity into consideration when your interest rate is established. You have checking accounts, deposit accounts, savings accounts, your merchant account, and possibly even a payroll account in your main bank. Make sure that your banker is basing your business value on your total relationship when setting your interest rate and loan terms.

  Banks make loans by balancing risk and reward. When you request a loan the bank identifies the risk, and appropriate collateral is required.

- Next comes the appropriate interest rate, and what should that be? The rate is a result of how much the loan costs the bank, the quality of the collateral, and the creditworthiness of the borrower (note that many banks will ask for a personal guarantee). If you have a deposit relationship with a bank, they will also take the availability of that cash into consideration when the rate is set. Keeping a clean set of business records and taxes will also come in handy.

  Remember that your bank does not pay for the use of the money that you keep in your checking account. Hopefully you will get some consideration for those funds. Show a consistent or growing average daily balance and you'll see your banker perk up and listen.

As long as you own a business you should be on a continual quest for a banking relationship that serves your company's financial interests and requirements. The bank that you choose today may not be the bank that you'll use in a year. Remember that you are their customer and when the time is right you should have several banks asking for your business. Don't ever forget that!

Insurance

In addition to having an ally at your bank, you'll also want to partner with an insurance agent. As a small-business owner, you may be able to use your personal relationship with your current agent to leverage good commercial insurance rates. As with your banking relationship, you are the insurance company's customer and should be treated as such.

You're going to want to be insured by a business owner's policy (BOP). When you're at your home office and holding a customer's device for service, the last thing you'll want to worry about is if something happened to that device while in your care. Theft, fire, vandalism—these are all real-world worries that all small business owners deal with. You can combat those worries to a certain degree with comprehensive insurance plans in place.

The most common types of commercial insurance are property, liability, and workers' compensation. In general, property insurance covers damages to your business property. Liability insurance covers damages to third parties. Workers' compensation insurance covers on-the-job injuries. Depending on your business, you may want additional specialized coverages. Listed below are some of the different types of business insurance.

Property Insurance

Property insurance pays for losses and damages to real or personal property. For example, a property insurance policy would cover fire damage to your office space. You can purchase additional coverages for business property, including:

- Glass Insurance. Glass insurance covers broken windows, including plate-glass windows.
- Inland Marine Insurance. Inland marine insurance covers property in transit and other people's property on your premises. For example, this insurance would cover shipping damage to customers' computers in transit to and from your office.
- Tenant's Insurance. Commercial leases often require tenants to carry a certain amount of insurance. A renter's commercial policy covers damages to improvements you make to your rental space and damages to the building caused by the negligence of your employees.
- Business Interruption Insurance. Business interruption insurance covers lost income and expenses resulting from property damage or loss. For example,

if a fire forces you to close your doors for two months, this insurance would reimburse you for salaries, taxes, rents, and net profits that would have been earned during the two-month period.

- Crime Insurance. Crime insurance covers theft, burglary, and robbery of money, securities, stock, and fixtures by employees and outsiders.

Liability Insurance

Liability insurance covers injuries that you cause to third parties. If someone sues you for personal injuries or property damage, the cost of defending and resolving the suit would be covered by your liability insurance policy. A general liability policy will cover you for common risks, including customer injuries on your premises. More specialized varieties of liability insurance include:

- Errors and Omissions Insurance. Errors and omissions ("E & O") insurance covers inadvertent mistakes or failures that cause injury to a third party. The act must actually be an inadvertent error, and not merely poor judgment or intentional acts. For example, an E & O policy would cover damages arising from an insurance agent failing to file policy applications, or a notary forgetting to fill out notarizations properly.
- Commercial Automobile Insurance. Commercial automobile policies cover the cars, vans, trucks, and trailers used in your business. The coverage will reimburse you if your vehicles are damaged or stolen or if the driver injures a person or property.

Workers' Compensation Insurance

Workers' compensation insurance covers you for an employee's on-the-job injuries. Businesses with employees are required by various state laws to carry some type of workers' compensation insurance. In most cases, workers' compensation laws prohibit the employee from bringing a negligence lawsuit against an employer for work-related injuries.

Keeping a Clean Customer Database

Let's briefly discuss your accounting software and your record-keeping (more to come on these topics in chapter 8). Put quite simply, you must understand that bookkeeping is a big part of the entire business success plan. Frankly, it's not a fun job and it can get quite monotonous at times, but clear and accurate records must be maintained.

The bookkeeping portion of any business can quickly become overwhelming if not consistently attended to, so a daily monitoring of the checking account balance will go a long way toward the discipline that needs to be maintained.

Within most account software programs one can keep records and copies of invoices, quotes, purchase orders, and other important business-related information that we will simply refer to as your customer database.

Your database record-keeping is just as important as your checking account record-keeping. In the end it all ties together and leaves a clear path as to where money is spent, why, how much, to whom, and from where. This is important as the Internal Revenue Service must have access to these clear records at a moment's notice. If they ever ask, you will need to show them where the money is or was that you've collected from your customers.

Not only for IRS reasons, you'll want to keep records of your customers and customer invoices in your database for your and their protection. It provides a clear sale date that will validate warranties and tie together inventory usage with sales numbers. The fact is that you need to keep this database active and correct because you won't be able to remember everything, even as smart as you are!

If you start your business and you use the customer database and invoicing features within your accounting software, you'll find this to be a safe and easy way to begin. However, you might quickly outgrow the limitations of said database—maybe you want your customers to be able to see their account and past orders through a website portal—which will require a new and possibly complicated solution. As your business grows, your customer database should change and evolve as needed.

Your First "Test" Order

Once you have your database set up, you'll need to add the products to your database and keep an inventory.

It's important for any business to keep track of and accurately account for the products you keep on hand. Keeping an accurate inventory is critical to lowering costs and providing an efficient process. When you first start out, keeping a "hand-count" of your inventory will suffice. Most likely, you'll only keep a few items on hand and have the ability to order replacement parts and service modules as you sell them to your customer. As your business grows, however, you'll soon want to institute some form of computerized inventory control and process.

The beauty of having a computerized inventory-management system is that it makes everything from inputting information to taking inventory much easier and much faster. Doing a hand count of a large inventory warehouse can take days, but a computerized inventory system can make the same process take just a couple of hours. In the case of your new computer repair shop, it may take only a matter of minutes in the beginning, which is a good thing!

Additionally, having a good inventory system will allow you to run reports so you can instantly see what you have on your shelves, how many of each product have been sold, and what needs to be reordered. Unfortunately having a computerized inventory system doesn't ensure accuracy, and the inventory data is only as good as the data that is being input into it. Taking sample counts and "having your finger on the pulse" of the inventory will help you feel more comfortable and allow you to rely more on the data that you accumulate.

What is the importance of having a correct inventory at the time of making your first test sale? It's simple. Each sale will most likely have a product attached to it. For example, let's say you installed a new hard drive into a Dell laptop computer. Ideally you'll have the parts and labor broken out (your customers will appreciate this), with the parts drawn directly from your inventory database so that your inventory remains correct. Once you sell a hard drive, you will have one removed from your inventory count, thus giving you one less to sell.

Mastering the Invoice

When you are ready to make a sample order, you should practice on family members. Have them sit in front of you and most typically you'll want to take their name, billing and shipping addresses, telephone number, and e-mail address. This will get the main points of their information into your system. Next, add the "service" that you'll be performing. For example, let's say you added 4 GB of memory to the order and a disk defragmentation service. Everything should be itemized and listed correctly. Once again your customers deserve to see the services that they are paying for and how much each costs without deciphering any type of "misc." descriptions.

Once you feel good about your invoicing (see sample invoices on pages 90 and 91) and your test order is appropriately deducting products from your inventory, you're ready to let the dogs out and you're one step closer to beginning business operations.

Mission Repair
19941 West 162nd Street
Olathe, KS 66062
(Toll-Free): 1-866-638-8402
Fax: 913-948-6991
HOURS - Central Standard Time
Monday - Friday   8:00 am - 6:00 pm
Saturday & Sunday 10:00 am - 5:00 pm
CLOSED MAJOR HOLIDAYS

INVOICE

Date:	Order#:
02/02/2013	**119631**

Order Comments:

Customer delivered a 15" MacBook Pro 1.67GHz.

Additional Information:

How did you hear about us? Google

Bill To: (Customer ID#1)   **Ship To:**

Ryan Arter   Ryan Arter
19941 West 162nd Street   19941 West 162nd Street
Olathe, KS 66062   Olathe, KS 66062
United States   United States
866-638-8402   866-638-8402
ryan@missionrepair.com

Payment Method: **Shipping Method:**

NONE   In-Store Pickup

Code	Description	Qty	Price	Total
Defrag	**Disk Defragmentation Service**	1	$46.99	$46.99

Subtotal:	$46.99
Tax (8.65%):	$4.06
Shipping & Handling:	$0.00
Grand Total:	**$51.05**

Refunds given if returned within 30 days of the date of purchase, shipping is not refundable.
Store credit will be issued if returned 31 - 90 days from the date of purchase.
After 90 days no refunds can be issued.

Mission Repair
19941 West 162nd Street
Olathe, KS 66062
(Toll-Free): 1-866-638-8402
Fax: 913-948-6991

HOURS - Central Standard Time
Monday - Friday   8:00 am - 6:00 pm
Saturday & Sunday 10:00 am - 5:00 pm
CLOSED MAJOR HOLIDAYS

INVOICE
Date: Order#:
02/02/2013   **119631**

Order Comments:

Customer delivered a 15" MacBook Pro 1.67GHz.

Additional Information:

How did you hear about us? Google

Bill To: (Customer ID#1)   **Ship To:**

Ryan Arter   Ryan Arter
19941 West 162nd Street   19941 West 162nd Street
Olathe, KS 66062   Olathe, KS 66062
United States   United States
866-638-8402   866-638-8402
ryan@missionrepair.com

Payment Method: **Shipping Method:**

 NONE   In-Store Pickup

Code	Description	Qty	Price	Total
922-8050	**4GB Memory for 15" MacBook Pro 1.67-2.4Ghz**	1	$49.99	$49.99
Service	**Service Labor for installation of Memory**	1	$42.50	$42.50
Defrag	**Disk Defragmentation Service**	1	$46.99	$46.99

Subtotal:	$139.48
Tax (8.65%):	$12.06
Shipping & Handling:	$0.00
Grand Total:	**$151.54**

Refunds given if returned within 30 days of the date of purchase, shipping is not refundable.
Store credit will be issued if returned 31 - 90 days from the date of purchase.
After 90 days no refunds can be issued.

Last but not least, you'll need to charge the appropriate sales tax on each order if required. While there are many counties around the country that don't require sales tax to be collected, most do, and you must charge and report it to the state in which you're operating.

Don't Forget the Sales Tax!

Sales tax is considered a "trust fund tax," meaning that you collect it and then you will need to send the collected tax to the state in which you operate, if required. I operate my businesses in the state of Kansas and I must collect sales tax in the county in which I operate for customers who take delivery at my offices.

There's a caveat to this sales tax issue and that is if I send a repaired device back to a customer within Kansas, I must charge the sales tax for the county of the customer's shipping address. This can make a mess of things quickly if I'm not careful.

Furthermore, if I ship a repaired device outside of the state of Kansas, I do not need to charge sales tax. It's the responsibility of all tax-paying Americans to report whether or not they purchased anything via mail order and then pay the tax directly to the state in which they live, if required.

Additionally, you cannot advertise or in any way indicate that the sales tax is being absorbed or paid by the business (you). However, you can include the sales tax in the price. If you sell a repair for $100 total and don't charge additionally for sales tax, you will need to post on the receipt to the customer that the purchase price includes sales tax, then you must pay that piece of the sales tax to your state.

The moral of the story is to get your sales tax right. It's not something you want to gloss over as it can get you into serious trouble as a retailer in your state.

How to Write a Quote

In business, a quotation is a document that you would give to a customer to describe specific necessary services that you suggest and their respective costs. Besides the term "quotation," it can also be referred to as a quote, proposal, bid, estimate, or tender.

You would normally prepare a quote upon request by a customer, and you can verbally quote your customer, but there are times when they are going to want it in writing.

Mission:Repair

19941 West 162nd Street
Olathe, Kansas 66062
1-866-638-8402
http://www.missionrepair.com

QUOTATION

Customer: John Doe
123 Main Street
Anytown, KS 66062

Date: 2/17/13

Description of Work	Amount
4GB Memory for 15" MacBook Pro 1.67GHz	$49.99
Installation Labor	$42.50
Disk Defragmentation Service	$46.99
Sub Total	$139.48
Tax	$12.06
Grand Total	**$151.54**

Remarks
Payment Terms: Credit Card or Personal Check
Validity: 7 days from the day of the quotation.
We trust that you will find our quote satisfactory and we look forward to working with you. Please contact us if you have any questions.

Ryan Art

By: Ryan Arter   Accepted By:

Your quote can be simple and can easily be performed in a word-processing program using your letterhead.

Start by having your business name, address, telephone number, and website address listed for contact. Next, clearly label the document as a quote, and add the date of the quote. Additionally, in the head of the document, add your customer name and address. List the services required, and then total the amount including tax, if applicable. Finally list your payment terms and the validity of the quote. For example, "This quote is valid for 7 days."

It's a great idea to personally sign the quote and leave space for your customer to sign the quote as well—as an acceptance. Quotes work especially well for businesses, and presenting firm pricing to the decision-making individual you're dealing with leaves a great impression.

Creating Purchase Orders

A purchase order is necessary for just about any company that sells products or needs to order parts and materials. The purchase order tells a vendor exactly what you need and the date you need the product in hand.

Depending on which software package you choose, you may have the capability to create purchase orders easily and seamlessly from within your program. You may also find that vendors prefer you to order directly off their own order form, or purchase form, so this may mean you'll need to keep your vendors organized well.

In all cases the purchase order (or P.O.) should have your business name, address, telephone number, e-mail address, and any other identifying information that will help your vendor identify you. Provide a shipping address if it's different from your billing address as well. Most vendors will require a unique purchase-order number that should also be listed at the top of the page.

The vendor's contact information should be present as well, including the vendor's business name, address, and telephone number. This will help you keep track of where you are making purchases and how much you are paying.

Next, list the products that you'd like to purchase along with the price that you've agreed to pay the vendor for said line items. Once this is completed, some vendors will require a signature by a company representative and then submission of the purchase order via e-mail or fax.

Mission Repair
19941 West 162nd Street
Olathe, KS 66062
(Toll-Free): 1-866-638-8402
Fax: 913-948-6991

HOURS - Central Standard Time
Monday - Friday   8:00 am - 6:00 pm
Saturday & Sunday 10:00 am - 5:00 pm
CLOSED MAJOR HOLIDAYS

Purchase Order #: 4755
Date: 11/28/2012
Customer Order #: N/A

From / Vendor:
eTech Parts
19939 W 162nd St
OLATHE, KS 66062
913-948-6990

Ship To:
Mission:Repair
19941 W 162nd St
Olathe, KS 66062

Ship Via: LOCAL
Due Date:

Terms:
FOB:

Code	Item	Qty	Price	Total
misc	GLASS DIGI TOUCH PANEL IPAD2	20	$32.63	$652.60

Subtotal: $652.60
Shipping Cost: $0.00
Grand Total: $652.60

Notes:

Signed By:

Time to Make a Sale

You're ready. Your website is up, and all you need to do is get an order. You check your watch, listen for the phone ... the days may even pass by like an eternity.

The key to getting your first sale is just a bit of patience. I remember my first "natural" sale. It was "natural" because it wasn't a friend or a neighbor who allowed me to input an invoice at cost just to test my system. It was a real sale from a real customer who thought I had the right business for the job.

What's even more exciting, and one hundred times more intimidating, is the first face-to-face customer. You might be sitting at your desk and see a strange car pull up in front of your window. You will be nervous, but it'll be time for you to experience a real live customer.

Your job will be to service that customer, and it's my advice to over-service when you can. Really drive it home. That first customer will always be your first customer, you can only have one. Make a good impression and you can only benefit from there. You need that first customer to tell a friend that your business was outstanding. If you maintain that mentality for every customer you ever have, you will be successful.

All right, the time is drawing near; it's almost time to open the doors and become a real live business performing real services. Don't get ahead of yourself just yet. There are a few more pieces to this puzzle that we need to address. Soon, very soon, you'll be sitting back watching the orders pour in, but the real success will be in the details.

For example, how much are you going to charge? This is going to be up for debate as long as you own your business, and take it from me, it is a question that you'll ask yourself as you progress in the years to come. There's a fine line between charging too much and losing business versus charging too little and losing profits.

While we're looking at pricing, let's also take a closer look at the services you are providing. Are you offering a full line of services that is broad enough to make an impression? If you focus on a niche, and I recommend that you do, make sure that you're covering the entire niche and not just a single product. Remember that success will be in the details and the finesse that you develop might only come with time and practice; however, let me give you some advice here before you cut the red ribbon and open the floodgates of business.

Determining Your Price

Determining your price can also be described as your "pricing strategy," which can be affected by many outside influences. As a business owner, you're going to want the most money for your work; you're really worth the price you're charging, right? Or are you?

With most new businesses this topic is a great challenge. We're going to take the logical step, and before we can determine which retail pricing strategy to use in setting the right price, we must know the costs associated with your services. The two main categories in factoring your service costs are the cost of goods (inventory) and the amount of operating expenses (your salary).

The cost of goods includes the prices paid for the parts that you will use in performing the services that you are offering, plus any shipping fees associated with the delivery of those parts. The cost of operating the business, or operating expenses, includes overhead, payroll, office supplies, marketing, and other business-related expenditures.

Regardless of the pricing strategy used, certainly don't go by what you "feel" will work, because the selling prices (the prices you will charge your customers) should more than cover the cost of obtaining the parts plus the expenses related to operating the business. You simply will not be able to remain in business if you charge too little to cover your expenses.

You will come to understand what your parts will actually cost—so you should then look at the competition for advice and see how they are pricing similar services and repairs. Also find the competitors that you feel are doing a good job and that seem to be successful (see chapter 10 for more about assessing the competition). One good indicator is to see how long your competition has been in business—nothing communicates success like longevity!

Your pricing strategy can be completed in one of several ways, but bear these ideas in mind:

Competitive Prices

Since your business is new, has no longevity, no customer base, no good reviews, no word of mouth, you may just have to be priced in such a way as to attract customers. There is nothing wrong with this approach, other than you make less money with each transaction and therefore it will take you longer to reach your financial goals. The good side of being competitive is that you will gain customers, which will give you a chance to get reviews and good word-of-mouth advertising—and you can always raise your prices when you're ready.

If you're going to price yourself below your competition, it's a good idea to also work on your vendors and negotiate the best pricing on your parts and really shop around for great deals on products that you will use to regain some of that lost margin.

Prestige Prices

You can take the opposite approach and if you have a good location or can offer some sort of upscale service that demands a higher price, you can justify being more expensive than your competition. If you guarantee same-day turnaround, offer a warranty that the other guys don't, or carry certifications or experience that can be great marketing material, then there's a possibility that you can be a white-glove service that can legitimately charge more for services.

Psychological Prices

You can use a bit of psychology to determine your prices as a way to allow your customers to perceive your pricing as fair by offering specials, deals, and value-added services that boost your service without incurring costs.

Another common method is odd-pricing figures that end in 5, 7, or 9. It is believed that consumers tend to round down a price of $9.95 to $9, rather than up $10.

I Love a Good Sale

I recently was in the market for a motorcycle jacket. I looked around online, but the prices of riding jackets were high enough to make me feel that I needed to try them on before I made a purchase, so I visited a local riding-apparel shop to take a look around.

It seemed that they were having a big sale, and I felt fortunate that I was in this particular shop at the right time.

Instead of a typical "50 percent off everything in the store" type of sale, they had select racks marked with advertisements that explained the product on the rack, the "normal price," and then the sale price listed below. The prices were about 50 percent off, but the way the marketing team had listed these "specials," it made me feel more like I was getting a good deal, versus the business just marking up their prices, then slashing them for this special event. I was truly enamored with their pricing.

So much in fact I bought a jacket, pants, and riding boots. The psychological pricing structure worked on me on that particular day, and I felt that I truly paid a fair price and was in the right place at the right time.

Loss-Leader Pricing

Services that are priced below your costs are referred to as loss leaders. Although this specific strategy may not make sense initially and you will make no money on these types of discounted services, the hope is that your customers will purchase other services from you at higher margins—now or in the future.

In the end, I would suggest that pricing be set to fair market value or slightly below, assuming that you are covering your costs. This gives you the opportunity to provide discounts that can be in the form of coupons, rebates, seasonal prices, or other promotional markdowns.

As you develop the best pricing model for your small business, understanding the ideal pricing strategy will depend on more than costs. It also depends on good pricing practices. It is difficult to say which components of pricing are most important, but keep in mind that the right price is the price the consumer is willing to pay, while providing you a profit.

Type of Services

Choosing the services for your business to sell may very well be the most difficult decision you will need to make before opening day. The choices may seem limitless and the task will likely be overwhelming at first. Not only should there be a demand for your service, but it must be profitable and something you enjoy working on. I know, you're in this to be a computer repair technician, but how many different computers are out there and what niche are you going to be a part of? Before you commit to a particular service line, consider the following factors while deciding what to offer your customers.

It's time to develop a baseline model price for your labor charges and use that model throughout your business. But how do you determine your hourly labor rate?

Since you're focusing on service, and you will need to charge for that service, you should post your hourly rate on your website and in your quotes when needed. The amount of your labor rate should be fair and reasonable and within the market standards. Many computer businesses that are starting up from home may be able to offer a lower cost per hour to their customers because overhead is low.

For example, starting from your home office, you can calculate how much you need to get paid per hour to keep your personal finances in check while making money to grow your business. If you need to make $20 per hour to survive, then you'd choose an hourly rate that is more than that and offer it to your customers.

There is a limit, however—you can't simply state "My hourly rate is $250 per hour," because you'll never get any clients by charging outrageous prices. This is a balancing act between you and your expenses. Charge too little and you'll never make it. Charge too much and you'll never make it. You need to find the sweet spot that attracts customers and keeps your cash flowing.

Marketability

It won't matter what services you sell if your customers aren't in need. Before considering what lines to offer, determine how you'll reach the market that you want to sell to. Once you know what kinds of customers you want, then you'll be able to determine their needs. A broad range will capture a larger audience, and the plan is to have enough customers who need your services to sustain your business. Your service selection doesn't have to appeal to all of the population but it should be something you can convince a large percentage of consumers they need. Take it from me, if you're going into the computer repair business, there's a lot of need.

Profit Margin

In a typical retail setting, selling big-ticket items is generally more profitable. When you look at the price of the services, don't forget to calculate direct and indirect costs (like overhead) of selling your goods. If you think you can sell ten iPod screen repairs a day for $100 each and the part costs you $50 each, it may look like you have a profit of $500 per day. But when you factor in your overhead expenses, that might average $400 per day, and you may find your profit isn't sufficient even though sales are good. Go after the highest profit margin services possible to give your business an edge that it needs.

Value-Added Service

Deliver a complete package for customers that offers more than the competition. Think about warranties and insurance plans, which are big in the market today. Customers will continue to come back to you to buy more. Additionally, satisfied customers are more open to recommendations for related products.

What's Popular

When it comes to selecting services to offer based on what's popular, timing is extremely important. New trends in electronics can be a great boost to your business, but you'll need to jump in at the beginning of the product life cycle in order to get the biggest bang for the buck. Learning to pick a hot product before it becomes hot is a valuable skill that comes from knowing your market, but training can be limited, so the risk of jumping into a service line that is relatively unknown should be weighed heavily before a snap decision is made.

Private Label

One way to guarantee a unique business is to have a private label. Your business touts your services (which include your processes, labor, and experience). This gives you an immediate advantage over other businesses that are simply distributing goods. There are other ways that you can take advantage of private labeling. Possibly partner with a small business that makes a product you would enjoy selling, and one that complements your services. Also consider private-label products that will allow you to brand an item made by another person with your business name. Now that's genius!

Quality

When deciding which services to sell in your store, ask yourself the following question: Would I offer this to my closest friend? If not, you may want to keep thinking about the types of services you offer. Product quality and your ability to provide competent services is extremely important when your reputation is on the line. Before you make any snap decisions and offer repairs that "might" fit your business, research and make educated decisions based on your technical confidence.

Diversity

It's my opinion that you should keep your service offerings simple in the beginning. If your line is narrow and focused, then your marketing efforts can be just as tightly focused, which will bring you the best results for your marketing budget. As your business grows, so can your service line as long as you keep new services compatible with your type of business, your location, and your market.

Some questions to keep in mind while selecting the types of services that you will offer upon opening your store:

- Would you use the service yourself if you were a consumer?
- Can you see yourself getting excited about this service?

- Would you sell it to someone you know?
- Is there a real need for the service in today's market?
- Can you imagine yourself selling this service for the next several years?

The key to having a successful business is to know your service line and to believe in the promise that you are selling. If you do not believe that you can deliver the service yourself, then you probably won't be successful at selling it and performing it for a total stranger. Keep brainstorming and you'll find the service line that meets both the needs of your target market and your own ability to deliver it.

Selling New Goods

OK, so we've talked a lot about computer repair, niches, types of repairs, and I've given you some ideas on how to get started. But let's complement your service line by offering a few items that you can profit from and help offset some costs associated with the service industry.

We've all been cross-sold to before. Think about "impulse buys" at the supermarket while waiting in line. You reach over, grab a pack of gum, and add it to your cart. It happens in retail stores across the country and there's a reason for it. Most likely, the cross-sell makes sense for us, whether we like the suggestions or not!

Cross-selling is selling an additional product to your existing customers, usually related to the service that you're currently performing or about to begin.

Cross-selling isn't difficult because you're selling to people who want to buy—it might just take a small suggestion for them to do so. The key, however, is to do it well. Here are a few tips on how to cross-sell to your customers effectively.

Suggest the Correct Product

Customers are more open to cross-purchasing if the products that you're suggesting are products they actually need. Suggesting a set of headphones to a customer who just had new software installed on a computer might not be the right fit. But a memory upgrade for that computer or a laptop carrying case would be.

We're also seeing more and more websites recommending "like" products (i.e., "Customers who purchased this item also looked at ..."). The idea is that users generally appreciate this thoughtful gesture.

Pick the Right Time

Customers tend to be very focused on your sales pitch, especially on the price when you're selling your services to them. Recommending additional expenses at that time may be ineffective. What you can do is recommend something to them once they've completed their sales call with you or have purchased online.

Show That You Care

Customers tend to be very sale or bargain focused. Having products in stock can certainly help your customers when they need it most. They are already feeling vulnerable, thinking of the expense of having their electronic device serviced, and if you perform "half" of what they need, they might feel slighted upon leaving your business. For example, let's say a customer brings a computer in for repair. You perform the repair, but then notice that the a/c adapter they own is failing. The customer comes to pick up the repaired computer only to be sent somewhere else to find an a/c adapter that will make the device work again.

If you had simply made a call, ordered an a/c adapter, and offered it to the consumer, you would have made an additional sale and additional, easy profits. You can even tell the customer, "I've ordered the correct a/c adapter for you; it will be here in a few days." The customer then thinks of your business as a "complete" service center that cares.

What does this all mean? I want you to think about stocking some of the most popular products that will complement your service line. New products are easy to sell in this instance and will be of great value when presenting a total package to your customers to solve their electronics problems. There's a fulcrum here that can tip against you; buying and stocking too much can gobble up your cash faster than you can imagine, so keep things simple to start!

These "impulse items" and extras are an excellent way to boost online sales and increase customer satisfaction. Bundle them with your services as options. Bundled products are usually cheaper than individual products bought separately. Recommending bundles will build trust with your customers (as you're helping them save money), hence increasing customer satisfaction.

Don't Be Pushy

No one likes a pushy salesperson, and I've never sold an item that I didn't think a customer really needed. Up-sells and cross-sells should be recommendations and not be forced on consumers. They sell themselves.

Here are a few appropriate phrases you can use on your website or in your sales pitches:

- Use "popular items" or "hot products" to show the items most popular among shoppers.
- Use "customers also bought" to highlight items that other people bought.
- Phrases such as "you might like" gives the power and choice to decide back to the users without imposing.

Cross-selling is relatively straightforward. Doing it well means that you'll not only sell more items, but you will also keep customers coming back to your site again and again. As you learn to cross-sell, maintain an inventory of new, warrantable products. You'll gain the ability to offer promotions and suggest items to customers who otherwise might need to visit a different business to make these purchases. Your goal is to keep the business in your control and in your store.

Selling Refurbished Inventory

Why even talk about refurbished inventory? Who wants to by a "used" anything? While this may be true for bathing suits (yuck!) there is a huge market for refurbished items and your new computer repair business is poised perfectly for this. Let's face it. The computer repair industry is the business of refurbishing. Once you repair a customer's computer, it's refurbished.

The definition from Merriam-Webster:

re·fur·bish
(tr) to brighten or freshen up: RENOVATE

So since you're in the business of refurbishing devices for customers, this puts you in the perfect spot to be the expert on selling refurbished products. Making extra money selling used items isn't new. But selling refurbished products can be a fun way to create a lucrative additional component to your business without having to come up with the capital that it takes to buy a stock of new items.

What's more, you could easily find a plethora of damaged and otherwise "junk" items on auctions sites like eBay for you to repair. Since you're repairing and refurbishing damaged or broken products, you're able to buy them at a small fraction of their worth when repaired. These low product costs make refurbishing and selling previously damaged goods one of the most profitable ways to make money with online or offline sales.

There are other advantages. You can have "new" and "refurbished" products in stock to give your customers a choice. Customers love options. If you can present them with an option that might save them money, you might get a sale that you would have otherwise not have made. Remember that psychological effect on consumers, like me? Special pricing on refurbished items are just the ticket that some customers are looking for and will appreciate.

07 Financial Planning & Management

Financial planning for your start-up business is the part of the process that determines whether or not your business is viable in the market, and it will be a key in determining whether or not your business plan is going to be able to attract the banker's attention if you decide to request start-up capital from the bank. More importantly, it will be the final word on whether or not you see the potential success for the financial investment you're about to make.

You can summarize your financial planning project by viewing three key financial reports.

1. Your income statement
2. Your cash-flow projection
3. Your balance sheet

You will need to create each of these three reports with all of the financial data that is required to start your business, and you'll start by reviewing your expenses. In fact, break up your expenses into two categories: your start-up expenses and your operating expenses.

Just as simply as it's stated, your start-up expenses are all of the costs that are involved in getting your business up and running. These will include:

- Your business license registration fees
- Starting inventory
- Office furniture
- Computer equipment
- Telephone equipment

This is just a small sample of start-up expenses; your own list will grow as you start gathering the data and writing it down as purchases are needed and made.

Operating expenses are the costs associated with keeping your business up and running. These are also called ongoing expenses and will show up consistently in your profit-and-loss statement. A short list of operating expenses may include:

- Monthly telephone fees
- Internet service
- Inventory
- Utilities
- Salaries
- Rent
- Consumable office materials
- Maintenance
- Shipping charges

Once again, this short, partial list gives you an idea and will get you started on the right foot. Once your operating expense list is accurate, you can add up the monthly running totals and see what it will cost you to operate your business each month.

Income Statement

Normally, established and operating businesses create an income statement once each quarter or even once a year, but for your new business you're going to want to create one each month for the first year.

A typical income statement will list the projected (or actual) sales, cost of goods sold, salaries, and all other expenses, with a total as a positive or negative number at the bottom.

A financial statement measures your company's financial performance each month and will tell you whether you're making or losing money—also known as the "bottom line." The financial performance is assessed by giving a summary of how much your business sells each month while subtracting all of the bills (expenses), showing you the end result: the net profit or loss. In my opinion, the income statement, otherwise known as the "profit-and-loss" statement or the "P&L," is an invaluable tool in determining the health of your business at a glance. See "P&L Statements: Numbers to Live By" later in this chapter.

Sample Expense Worksheet

NEWCO, LLC STARTUP EXPENSES WORKSHEET

Expense	Cash Budgeted
Accounting Services	$100.00
Advertising	$250.00
Cash	$100.00
Equipment - CPU	$829.00
Equipment - Tools	$190.00
Equipment - Bench	$520.00
Insurance	$139.00
Internet Service	$62.00
Legal Costs	$100.00
Office Supplies	$300.00
Rent	$1,215.00
Software	$500.00
Starting Inventory	$1,830.00
Telephone Service	$88.00
Website Service	$99.00
Total Startup Costs	**$6,322.00**

Cash-Flow Projection

The cash-flow projection shows you how your cash is expected to flow in and out of your business; it does not measure how much you are making. Also, don't confuse a cash-flow projection with a cash flow statement. The projection shows the anticipated usage of the money in your account, while the statement shows the actual use of the money.

For example, cash coming into your business consists of sales in the form of checks, credit card charges, etc. Cash is the payment that your customers make to you, even though they may not necessarily pay in actual dollar bills.

Cash going out of your business is all of your expenses, such as rent, telephone bills, inventory, shipping supplies, etc.

NEWCO, LLC: Income Statement Projection January through December 2014

Ordinary Income/Expense [Jan 1 – Dec 1]	
INCOME	
Sales	$2,979,128.92
Total Income	$2,979,128.92
Cost of Goods Sold	
Cost of Goods Sold	$1,068,709.96
State Sales Tax Paid	$24,214.27
Total COGS	$1,092,924.23
Gross Profit	$1,886,204.69
EXPENSE	
Advertising	
Parade	$326.66
Television	$67,080.20
Total Advertising	$67,406.86
Automobile Expense	$5,180.14
Bank Service Charges	$1,004.36
Contract Labor	$1,500.75
Credit Card Fees	$58,261.66
Delivery Service	$115.57
Dues and Subscriptions	$1,731.18
Fees	$35.00
Insurance	
Business Auto	$5,146.18
Health	$45,568.05
Liability Insurance	$658.32
Work Comp	$995.67
Total Insurance	$52,368.22
Interest Expense	$1,709.06
Marketing	
Affiliate Commissions Paid	$1,971.04
Supplies	$754.29
Internet	$258,356.97
Total Marketing	$261,082.30
Office Supplies	$14,031.70

continued

Payroll Expenses		
Add to W-2 at end of year		$2,000.00
Payroll Processing Fee		$2,942.16
Simple IRA Match		$6,817.63
Taxes		$66,975.61
Wages		$667,904.18
Total Payroll Expenses		$746,639.58
Penalties & Fees		$830.46
Postage and Delivery		$3,332.97
Professional Development		$300.00
Professional Fees		
Accounting		$9,172.50
Legal Fees		$4,128.75
Total Professional Fees		$13,301.25
Promotions		$3,084.11
Rent		$31,051.97
Repairs		
Building Repairs		-$2,883.22
Janitorial Exp		$3,198.74
Total Repairs		$315.52
Shipping		
Freight		$477,068.04
Supplies		$7,036.30
Shipping - Other		-$54.20
Total Shipping		$484,050.14
Storage		$3,777.46
Taxes		
Property		$304.56
Total Taxes		$304.56
Telephone		$33,243.85
Travel & Ent		
Entertainment		$12,723.36
Meals		$1,893.89
Parking		$103.00
Travel		$5,113.77
Total Travel & Ent		$19,834.02

continued

Utilities		
Alarm		$3,238.53
Gas and Electric		$4,872.69
Internet		$2,288.90
Trash		$583.78
TV Service		$1,525.09
Water		$138.00
Total Utilities		$12,646.99
TOTAL EXPENSE		$1,817,139.68
Net Ordinary Income		$69,065.01
Net Income		**$69,065.01**

Think of "cash flow" as money "flowing" in and out of your checking account. If more money is flowing into your checking account, you're in a "positive cash flow" position and you can pay all of your bills. If more cash is flowing out of your account and you become close to overdrawing your account, this puts you into a "negative cash flow" position. This is why you invest in your business with start-up capital, or cash. Most businesses don't instantaneously start producing positive cash flow from day one. You, as the owner and sole investor, provide the up-front cash to give the business the positive cash flow it needs to operate from day one.

If you don't have enough cash to cover the negative position, then you can ask for investors or consult your banker. Not having enough cash to start a business is why new businesses typically ask for a loan or a line of credit from their bank. It's to cover shortages in their cash flow.

A typical cash-flow projection will list the carried cash from the previous month, add in projected sales for the month, and then list all of the actual expenses anticipated for the month. This will in the end deliver a balance that is carried over to the month thereafter.

I like the cash-flow projection because it gives you a snapshot, month after month, of the positive or negative position your business may be in and allows you to see into the future and make adjustments. For a bank loan officer, the cash-flow projection offers evidence that your business is a good credit risk and that there will be enough cash on hand to make your business a good candidate for a line of credit or short-term loan.

Balance Sheet

Your balance sheet is the last of the three financial statements that you need to complete your financial plan. It will provide a snapshot of your business's net worth at a particular point in time. It summarizes all the financial data about your business, breaking it into three sections:

1. Assets
2. Liabilities
3. Equity

The assets of the business are tangible objects that have some sort of financial value and that are owned by the company. A liability is a debt that is owed. Equity is the net difference when the liabilities are subtracted from the total assets. Normally, your business will create and execute a balance sheet once per year, usually at tax time.

After reviewing and analyzing each of these three (accurate) statements, you can then legitimately assess and review your financial plan. These documents will tell you without a shadow of a doubt whether you have a viable business enterprise or a doomed venture that never has a chance to get off the ground. In all respects, you'll be looking for positive numbers rather than negative ones to give you a quick glimpse at the future.

What if your statements come out negative and show financial destruction? It's up to you to decide, but I would cut expenses. I ran into this very problem and rather than give up, I cut expenses. Maybe you don't need a new desk. Cut it. Maybe you can't take a salary for the first couple of months. Cut it. Maybe there's a cheaper vendor that can help you reduce your inventory costs? Find it.

There's also another way to offset the negative numbers. Sell more. The more sales you have, the more positive things will be. I've said it before and I'll say it again, and this is especially true in the beginning: "Fight for every sale." This doesn't mean that you need to subject your customers to a high-pressure sales game. "Fight for every sale" means that you need to do your best, go above and beyond, and make sure the customer is happy. Make more money and the negatives dwindle. Make enough money and your financial problem will be nonexistent.

Sample Cash-Flow Projection

TWELVE-MONTH CASH FLOW NEWCO, LLC

	Pre-Startup EST	Jan-13	Feb-13	Mar-13	Apr-13	
Cash on Hand (beginning of month)		5,500	2,141	562	3,513	
CASH RECEIPTS						
Cash Sales	0	5,000	10,000	15,000	20,000	
Collections fm CR accounts	0	0	0	0	0	
Loan/other cash inj.	10,000	0	0	5,000	0	
TOTAL CASH RECEIPTS	10,000	5,000	10,000	20,000	20,000	
Total Cash Available (before cash out)	10,000	10,500	12,141	20,562	23,513	
CASH PAID OUT						
Purchases (merchandise)	1,830	2,000	4,000	8,000	8,000	
Purchases (shipping)	0	250	670	1,340	2,010	
Purchases (packaging)	250	250	300	350	400	
Gross wages (exact withdrawal)	0	0	500	1,000	1,000	
Payroll expenses (taxes, etc.)	0	0	60	120	120	
Outside services	0	250	250	250	250	
Supplies (office & oper.)	0	300	300	300	300	
Repairs & maintenance	0	100	200	300	300	
Advertising	0	250	250	250	250	
Car, delivery & travel	0	1,100	1,100	1,100	1,100	
Accounting & legal	200	200	200	200	200	
Rent	1,215	1,215	1,215	1,215	1,215	
Telephone	88	88	88	88	88	
Utilities	216	216	216	216	216	
Insurance	139	139	139	139	139	
Taxes (real estate, etc.)	0	0	0	0	0	
Interest (see below)	0	0	0	0	0	
Other expenses (Internet)	62	250	250	250	250	
Other (credit card fees)	0	90	180	270	360	
Other (specify)						
Miscellaneous	500	500	500	500	500	
SUBTOTAL	4,500	7,198	10,418	15,888	16,698	
Loan payment plus interest	0	1,161	1,161	1,161	1,161	
Capital purchase (specify)	0	0	0	0	0	
Other startup costs						
Reserve and/or Escrow						
Owners' Withdrawal						
TOTAL CASH PAID OUT	4,500	8,359	11,579	17,049	17,859	
Cash Position (end of month)	5,500	2,141	562	3,513	5,654	

ay-13	Jun-13	Jul-13	Aug-13	Sep-13	Oct-13	Nov-13	Dec-13	Total Item EST
5,654	7,495	10,526	14,627	19,798	27,159	34,470	39,941	39,941
5,000	30,000	35,000	40,000	45,000	50,000	50,000	50,000	
0	0	0	0	0	0	0	0	
0	0	0	0	0	0	0	0	
5,000	30,000	35,000	40,000	45,000	50,000	50,000	50,000	
),654	37,495	45,526	54,627	64,798	77,159	84,470	89,941	
),000	12,000	14,000	16,000	18,000	20,000	20,000	20,000	
,680	3,350	4,020	4,690	5,360	6,030	6,700	6,700	
450	500	550	600	650	700	750	800	
,000	3,000	4,000	5,000	5,000	7,000	8,000	9,000	
360	360	480	600	600	840	960	1,080	
250	250	250	250	250	250	250	250	
300	300	300	300	300	300	300	300	
300	300	300	300	300	300	300	300	
500	1,500	1,500	1,500	1,500	1,500	1,500	1,500	
,100	1,100	1,100	1,100	1,100	1,100	1,100	1,100	
200	200	200	200	200	200	200	200	
,215	1,215	1,215	1,215	1,215	1,215	1,215	1,215	
88	88	88	88	88	88	88	88	
216	216	216	216	216	216	216	216	
139	139	139	139	139	139	139	139	
0	0	0	0	0	0	0	0	
0	0	0	0	0	0	0	0	
250	250	250	250	250	250	250	250	
450	540	630	720	810	900	900	900	
500	500	500	500	500	500	500	500	
,998	25,808	29,738	33,668	36,478	41,528	43,368	44,538	0
,161	1,161	1,161	1,161	1,161	1,161	1,161	1,161	
0	0	0	0	0	0	0	0	
,159	26,969	30,899	34,829	37,639	42,689	44,529	45,699	0
,495	10,526	14,627	19,798	27,159	34,470	39,941	44,242	0

NEWCO, LLC: BALANCE SHEET   After 1st Month of Business

ASSETS	
Current Assets	
Checking/Savings	
Checking Account	5,821.00
Savings Account	900.00
Petty Cash	100.00
Total Checking/Savings	6,821.00
Total Current Assets	6,821.00
Fixed Assets	
Computer Equipment	829.00
Furniture & Fixtures	520.00
Inventory	1,830.00
Total Fixed Assets	3,179.00
Total Assets	**10,000.00**
LIABILITIES & EQUITY	
Liabilities	
Current Liabilities	
Accounts Payable	
Accounts Payable	4,272.21
Total Accounts Payable	4,272.21
Credit Cards	
AmEx Gold	800.42
Visa	142.87
Bank Credit Card	958.62
Total Credit Cards	1,901.91
Other Current Liabilities	
Sales Tax Payable	938.59
Total Other Current Liabilities	938.59
Total Current Liabilities	7,112.71
Total Liabilities	**7,112.71**
Equity	
Common Stock	0.00
Distributions to Owner	-1,000.00
Opening Bal Equity	0.00
Retained Earnings	0.00
Net Income	3,800.00
Total Equity	**2,800.00**
TOTAL LIABILITIES & EQUITY	9,912.71

Yes, keeping expenses down is a good plan. Getting your sales revenues up is better.

P&L Statements: Numbers to Live By

As a business owner, I find myself constantly looking at my "numbers." This can mean a lot of things. As a creature of habit, I routinely look at my bank accounts (personal and business) as the first task of the day. Once again, trying to keep a close rein on my expenses and knowing what my cash position is at all times is extremely important.

In my opinion, knowing your cash position is the beginning of the picture to knowing your business health. There are other things like your forecasted sales, your daily sales, your accounts receivable and payable, but there's also the holy grail of business reports, which I consider to be the profit-and-loss statement.

The profit-and-loss statement (aka P&L) is the result of the immaculate accounting procedures that you have in place. Most accounting programs include an automatic P&L feature that can slice and dice the numbers for you in a matter of minutes. In a nutshell, your P&L will give you a quick snapshot of the health of your business for the last day, week, or month. Truth be told, to truly evaluate a P&L, it should be looked at over a year, as payments and receivables take time to make the account statements. Looking at your P&L over a one-week period is not a good idea. It's better used as more of a long-term gauge when you are trying to assess your moneymaking abilities.

Have you ever heard the idiom "That's the bottom line" or "What's the bottom line"?

This is originally a business term and is referring to the last line on any business P&L statement. "The bottom line" is the number that is calculated from all of your sales versus all of your expenses and is the calculation in positive or negative numbers.

"The bottom line" is the true answer to whether or not your business is making money. When the last line of your P&L statement is a positive number, that's the amount of money your business has made for the duration of the report. If the last line of your P&L statement is a negative number, then that's the amount of money your business has lost.

In the beginning, it's difficult to maintain a positive bottom line. Expenses are typically high while sales are typically low. There are exceptions to this rule but be prepared for a negative P&L to start. Many business analysts accept that it may take years for your small business to make money; while this may be true, I do not consider this a rule. As a small business owner I am in the game to make money. I watch my P&L, which will describe each expense in detail at the push of a button. Just when you forgot that you spent $200 last month on business lunches, that will pop back up on your P&L, which may trigger a new look at expensing meals until the profits rise. In fact, had you not spent the $200 on those lunches, your bottom line would be $200 greater . . . unless that $200 in expense landed you a large project that you wouldn't have received otherwise.

The point is that with your P&L, you can watch your business, watch your expenses, and keep track of the health of the business month to month. I find great satisfaction in viewing my P&L statements year after year. Watching the bottom line grow from a negative to a positive is proof that you're doing something right. The other side of the coin is that if you see it in the negative, it's not time to panic. Take into account your cash position, your sales leads, and your current expenses and make the necessary adjustments.

Personal Credit versus Business Credit

There will be a time when credit plays a part in your business. It's important to establish a business credit report that is different from your personal credit report.

As a business owner, you have the unique ability to establish and build credit for yourself and your business. It's great news if you're trying to grow your company, so you don't have to rely solely on your personal credit every time credit is needed. Keeping them separate will remove the headaches when you need your personal credit to work on your behalf, for example if you buy a new house.

Your personal credit is established and linked to your Social Security number. Associated with your number is a credit report that fluctuates with every credit check, new account added, or late payment that you make. As you progress in life and want to use your credit to buy a new house, then you'll want your credit report to show that you're a responsible citizen and show creditors that you have the ability to pay back a debt.

In the business world, when one business issues credit to another business, it's called trade credit. Fun fact: Trade credit is the single largest source of lending in the world.

Your trade-credit transactions, if formally conducted, are gathered by the business-credit bureaus to create your business-credit report using your business name and EIN (Employer Identification Number) that you receive from the IRS.

If you're asking another business directly for credit, they can view your business-credit report with the EIN and see your creditworthiness. The major credit bureaus that compile and provide copies of your business-credit reports are Experian, Equifax, Dun and Bradstreet, and Business Credit USA.

There is one small flaw with business-credit reporting, and that is the information given to them is voluntary. That is to say that the business extending you credit must formally report your on-time payments to the reporting agencies for your payments to positively affect your credit. The flaw is that they are not required to do so. It's the same if you extend a customer net terms—you don't need to report the timeliness of their payments to anyone.

It's a fact that most businesses won't report your good or bad credit ratings, and you might run for years on trade credit with your vendors and never show any movement on your business credit report. So why even try?

There are statistics about average Americans and their credit, and a typical American has one hard credit check per year and eleven open accounts. If a business owner, such as yourself, merely uses personal credit for all business activities, there will be more credit checks and likely more accounts with debt on the personal credit report, theoretically lowering the personal credit score. This will make it harder to obtain personal credit when needed.

The solution is to use your EIN to keep your personal credit out of business activities as much as possible.

1. Assuming that you have your EIN, go register it with the business-credit bureaus and comply with their requirements. Some of them are simple, like having a dedicated telephone number for your business. Don't offer any red flags and be as thorough as possible.
2. Have your business plan available. It's often asked for by businesses that offer credit.
3. Find a vendor that will offer you trade credit without a personal credit guarantee.
4. Ask that vendor to report the payment records to the credit bureau to help you build your business-credit report.

5. Make sure you don't make late payments.

6. Continue to accrue debts and then subsequently make payments each month to keep your business-credit profile current. Pay them off each month if possible.

It's in your best interest to begin early and get your business credit started off on the right foot. It's a simple process, it's a benefit of being your own boss, and it can keep the personal side of your credit as clean as that of the average American out there—but we all know that the business owner is anything but average!

Vendor Relationships

This is a big topic and businesses can be made or broken by their vendor relationships. I classify the important vendors as the suppliers you buy your inventory from. A predictable, honest, and reliable vendor goes a long way in helping your company succeed. In the process, the vendor succeeds as well, so this relationship can easily be looked at as a win-win situation.

You'll want to choose carefully. In the beginning, you won't have any "relationships." So shop around for your inventory with as many vendors as you can find. What makes a good vendor? Someone who sells reliable items at a great price who will stand behind those products in the event of an issue. The vendor should be knowledgeable about the products and also know about industry trends and rumors that may be floating around. A good vendor source can give you the edge over the competition in terms of information.

As you establish good relationships, I encourage you to continue to shop around. It gives you a chance to "test" your vendor and keep him or her honest. Once you have an established account, and then stop ordering because you found a cheaper price somewhere else, a good vendor will react and retain your business.

When you're working with vendors, remember that they are working for you. That's to say, you're their customer, so it's protocol for you to demand that they keep their promises and deliver excellent support. Your customers will demand the same of you, right?

A good vendor is easy to do business with. When placing an order, you'll be able to count on the fact that the product you're looking for is in stock and will ship with a turnaround time you're used to receiving. If there are any hiccups in the process, the vendor will contact you immediately and give you a solution.

At the same time, communicate with your vendors, stay professional, and treat them with the respect that they deserve. Since you're going to be running a professional, well-respected business there's no reason to not treat your vendors as you would want to be treated. In the long run, you will find that vendors will help you, the calm, reasonable customer, before they go out of their way to help the unreasonable one.

The bottom line is that the better the relationship between your business and your vendors, the more concessions they will make. If your sales skyrocket and you start spending hundreds of thousands of dollars each year with vendors, they will give you better pricing, which in turn leads to more profits, which leads to more money available for advertising, which leads to more sales and more items you'll need to order from your vendor.

How to Get Net Terms

It can't hurt to ask. New businesses without a credit history are the highest risk. You may want to introduce yourself and your business directly to either the business owner or the credit department manager of the supplier you would like to do business with. Offer to show the decision maker your business plan and explain that you need your first order on credit in order to launch your service business. The vendor you're looking at may have terms available to new businesses or simply grant you an account based on your open conversation and honesty.

The idea behind trade credit is to have goods shipped to your business and sell them before you have to pay for them. One of the best tools for slowing cash outlay of your new business is the trade credit available from some suppliers. Trade credit is one part of the process to build business credit. It is an open account with a vendor who lets your business buy now and pay later. There are other ways to finance your inventory, but most include having to pay interest on a loan. This is why trade credit is key in reducing the amount of working capital needed.

Many suppliers may require the first order (or even several orders) to be paid by credit card until your business has been deemed creditworthy. Once a relationship has been established and a vendor feels that your business can pay its bills on time, it is possible to negotiate open credit and terms with your suppliers.

New customers such as your business may need to fill out a credit application and provide some other financial information about the business. Other items found on a credit application could include:

- Company name, address, contact information
- Business structure: corporate, partnership, sole proprietor, etc.
- Terms requested
- Sales-tax number
- Tax EIN
- DUNS number
- Years in business
- Annual revenue
- Bank information
- Credit-card number
- Trade references of other suppliers
- Signature of an authorized officer

In all cases, buy only what you need in the beginning so you can ensure that you pay your bills on time. You will want to keep open credit terms with your vendors, and some of them may become as dependent on you for the success of their business as you are on them!

Buy Low & Make a Profit

Speaking of credit with vendors, as a customer you should always be on the lookout for suppliers who offer not only the lowest prices, but also fast, dependable delivery. Try not to become too committed to one vendor because it offers credit terms to your business. In the long run this is not the right way to handle your profits.

Find a vendor who is willing to negotiate your purchases, especially if you're repeatedly ordering from the same vendor. Again, as a customer you will have some weight with the vendor and as your purchase volumes go up, your price should be driven down. I once had a boss who said, "It's not the sales price that makes the money, it's the price at which you buy the product." Basically, buy right.

Don't let the lure of net terms sway you from the real answer, which is to make money. If you have to pay COD or prepay to get a better price, in the long run it might just be the answer that changes your perspective and profitability.

Cash Your First Paycheck

So you've gotten your first sale, you've performed a few repairs, and you have the ability to write yourself a check. This will come with a lucrative run of services and your feeling of success and getting a hold of your business structure.

You'll never forget your first paycheck, and if you are like me, you needed it (although it was insignificant compared to the bills I had accumulated). What it did for me was motivate. When I had the ability to actually take an income from my business, it drove me to work harder. I realized that I was in control of my destiny and my success or failure was solely upon my shoulders. I chose to push through the tough times and live as frugally as possible. The time for living like a rock star was not imminent in the beginning (nor is it now, to be truthful) but it's about setting goals and sticking to a plan, even if that plan is to be flexible.

Establishing a successful small business can build credibility and allow you to network through the business community, which will be hugely valuable when launching your next business start-up (now is the time to think about that too!). But while you're juggling all of these tasks, be careful not to get too comfortable with a steady paycheck. Only time will tell, and as the business owner, your pay is 100 percent dependent on the profit of the business.

08

Taxes & Record-Keeping

Bookkeeping in small business is not usually complex, but for some reason, the thought of recording transactions and reviewing financial statements strikes fear in new business owners. The truth of the matter is that as a business owner, you should be focused on selling the product or service you are offering, networking, and making the contacts every successful business does. Accounting is a detail-oriented and sometimes time-consuming process to ensure all company transactions are being recorded properly. For this, hiring a bookkeeper or accountant is usually advised for small businesses that can afford the usual hundred dollars a month most small-business accountants will charge for basic services.

The bottom line is that you want to stay out of trouble with the IRS and off their radar by providing complete, timely, and accurate taxes and records. Since this is not my forte, I leave it up to the professionals.

Accounting

Accounting, by far, is one of the most important aspects of starting up and operating a business. It's so easy to get caught up in the more glamorous start-up tasks of designing your website or choosing a business name, yet without a solid understanding of the numbers you will not survive.

Far too many business owners are overwhelmed with the accounting piece of a business because for most entrepreneurs this is not their area of expertise. There is the choice of immediately hiring a trained professional to maintain the company books, but even if you do so there's much to be gained by learning about your business accounting methods. Personally, I always want to know whether my businesses are making money at any given time, and without correct and complete accounting records, a business owner may think that the enterprise is profitable when it is not.

Over 28 percent of businesses declaring bankruptcy cite problems with the financial structure of the company as the main cause of failure, according to a Small Business Administration study, "Financial Difficulties of Small Businesses and Reasons for Their Failure." Take the responsibility of entrepreneurship by learning the basics of accounting.

Methods of Accounting

There are only two generally accepted accounting methods: cash and accrual accounting. Small businesses have the option of choosing between these two, while other businesses are legally required to use the accrual method.

The accrual method shows your real-time financial health, and most accounting software packages simplify the process of accrual accounting. Moving from the cash system to accrual can be as easy as checking a box in your accounting software, which will do the rest for you. However, if you run a simple, low-revenue business, don't feel pressured to adopt the accrual system. I started my business on a cash basis, and it has proven to be the right decision for me.

Keep Your Options Open; You're in Control

I started my business with an accountant recommended by my lawyer. I quickly realized that he wasn't the right accountant for me. He belittled my business and told me I was doing things wrong.

It was a difficult thing to hear especially when I was burdened with the curses of a start-up company.

I soon replaced him with another accountant who was on the same page as I was: one who understood the value of what I was bringing to the market, my goals in the business, my growth plan, and my willingness to collaborate.

Remember that you can pick your team of professionals you surround yourself with, and you should feel safe and secure with the decisions you make. Don't be afraid to make changes along the way, especially with regard to accounting. It's your money and you need to know that it's being handled right.

Hiring an Accounting Pro

Unless you are a numbers whiz or have a degree in accounting, you will need to employ the services of a professional to set up your accounting software. To get a grasp on your small-business accounting and financials, should you hire a bookkeeper or an accountant?

It's typical for a small business owner to interview and hire a part-time bookkeeper to assist in starting the company records and even maintaining the books and bank accounts on a weekly (or as-needed) basis. Bookkeeping can be a mundane task that can tie you up from the business of growing your business.

Hiring a certified public accountant (CPA) makes good sense for growing companies, businesses with more complex business structures (such as limited liability companies), and when you add employees to your company.

Initially, you may start your business part-time or at home to keep expenses low. The cost of an accountant on a monthly basis can be too much for a one-person business. Either prepare the books yourself or have a bookkeeper involved in the process. Use the accountant for your year-end tax planning. For years I have personally used my accountant at tax time, and we conference throughout the year to make sure we are moving in the right direction. The peace of mind of having an accountant in the background is well worth it.

When you do plan to hire an accountant or bookkeeper, remember to find one you can trust and build a solid relationship with because you need his or her advice and guidance in steering your business now and in the future.

At the end of each day, your account and financial snapshot should be complete and correct. Keep a clean and balanced business checking account. Know your financial limits. Keeping your books and accounting right will translate across your entire business model. It also keeps you legal and out of trouble at tax time.

Federal & State Taxes

Death and taxes. Two things we cannot avoid.

Here we go with some serious topics, and it's best to refer to your CPA on these matters for the final verdict. However, there are some general guidelines that you're going to face as you progress down the business ownership road. When starting your business, you will decide on what form of entity it will be. Sole proprietorship? LLC? Corporation?

Certified Public Accountants Are Your Best Friends

As I've mentioned, the best reason to hire or retain a CPA is for peace of mind. However, there are some real functions that a CPA can perform that you may not be able to. The duties of a CPA will vary depending on your business's financial health and tax needs, but most businesses can use the help of CPAs. For the most part, CPAs are responsible for ensuring that your company stays on budget and makes as much money as possible throughout the year. CPAs are also responsible for filing taxes for a company and advising owners about potential investment opportunities or financial shortcomings. Most CPAs must attend classes or seminars related to tax law so they can stay as up to date on that information as possible. This could happen once a year or once a month, but I would be willing to bet that it's more often than you or I read up on tax law.

CPAs will most likely work from their office, offsite from your business. If you get to the point where you need to hire a full-time CPA, you're on a fast track to success! Most large-scale corporations need in-house accountants to keep track of their finances, but small businesses typically outsource the needed work to local entities.

Typical CPAs have a list of clients they service on a regular basis and as years pass, you and your CPA will be best friends. I don't necessarily mean in a literal, social context; however, I am sure that many true friendships have been born between business owner and accountant.

I mean "best friends" in more of a business sense. When you get to the point where your CPA saves you money, shows you how he saves you money, and then proves how he'll continue to save you money, you'll think differently about him. It's all comes down to the mighty dollar in a small business, and your CPA is on your side. A good CPA can often easily pay for himself in tax savings found and recovered.

Once you do, this will determine which income tax return you will need to file each year. Additionally, the federal government has four basic types of business taxes that must be paid:

- Income tax
- Self-employment tax
- Employer payroll taxes
- Excise tax

There are volumes written on this subject and you should do as much research as you can but know this: There's a price to pay for legally owning and operating a business in the United States. Understanding and believing that paying your taxes is the right thing can be the beginning of a successful enterprise. That doesn't mean you shouldn't take legal advantages when you can; let your CPA find those for you.

Nearly every state imposes some sort of business or corporate income tax. Like federal taxes, your state will impose taxes based on the structure of your business. While a lesser of two evils, state taxes will be collected and you will sleep well knowing that you're doing your part in keeping the country great . . . by paying your taxes.

Expense Reports & Receipts

You will have receipts. If you do a good job at keeping your personal finances in line, then you're off to a good start with your business. If you're sloppy with your personal accounts, it's time to straighten up and get a good system in place.

Receipts will come with every purchase you make at your business, from ordering inventory (sometimes called invoices), to ordering a telephone system, to putting gas in the company vehicle. You will have a pile of receipts.

You will need to sort out how these receipts are to be categorized in your accounting system. This is the beginning of getting an accurate P&L statement, because if you just classify all of your receipts under the "misc" category, you won't know where in the business you are making or losing money. Keep your receipts in a common place, such as a paper bin, file folder, or even a coffee can. You will then be able to refer to them as you balance your checkbook in your accounting software and classify them correctly.

Most likely there will be times when you use your business funds for personal use. I mean, it's your business, right? Well, that's OK, but you will need to claim personal-use receipts as income, rather than expenses. Yes, this can get complicated.

Additionally, you may take business trips. If you plan on reimbursing yourself upon your return from a business trip, I suggest the use of expense reports for these occasions. You should report each expense under the specific date when the expenditure occurred. Automobile mileage or flight expenses should be reported on the specific days of departure and return. For example, you should record the expense of your departure flight on the day you leave, then write down the price of the return trip when you return. Record all expenses in succession on the expense report. It helps to arrange your receipts by day ahead of time, which can save you time. You will need to write in specific dates on the expense report, as these spaces are usually blank. Finally, add the sums of daily expenses vertically, then calculate your totals for each type of expense horizontally. Subtract any advance payments you may have taken from the business (i.e., cash) from those that are due you and write yourself a reimbursement check.

Make sure you double-check your calculations before filing your expense report. And as usual, refer to your CPA for specific instructions to create a personalized plan for you and your business.

Paper Files: A Necessity

There just is no substitution for a good old-fashioned paper filing system; however, we have come a long way in the business world in the direction of a paper-free workplace. I suggest that you keep what you must keep and shred the rest.

If you're worried about pitching documents that may be needed at some point, you're not alone—many home-business owners decorate the living room with archive storage boxes or large file cabinets stuffed with old bank statements, tax returns, and pay stubs. (All right, maybe you keep this stuff in the garage or in a storage facility!) But as your CPA finishes up your tax returns this year, take the opportunity to organize your paper files and keep them neat. You must keep copies of your tax returns, your business licenses, all of your receipts, and basically anything that has your original signature on it. But if you're willing to use online banking and create a digital archive of crucial records (I always keep a digital file of my employee's records), you can go paperless in a lot of ways to help save the environment.

Do yourself a favor, though, and if you do "clean house" and think about tossing all of those old bank statements, invest in a paper shredder to protect your identity.

The thought of going "paperless" is no longer a distant dream for small businesses. New and changing technology has provided us with some tools that we need to transition the clutter in our businesses to a digital, online format. It really doesn't mean that going paperless is easy to do, however, and I personally still have a need for an original signature at times.

The major con of the paperless environment is data failure. Yes, a digital copy of your employee's resume is quick to find and see, but it can be gone or become corrupted just as quickly. If you're going to go paperless, that means there will be extra expense investing in an additional redundant backup system that will keep all of those files safe and protected. While you're at it, that system should be housed in a second location for security reasons.

Speaking of security, digital files are susceptible to online or network "attacks." A paper file can never be seen by prying online eyes because a computer hacker cannot break through your firewall, crack your computer password, and then open a locked filing cabinet in your office to read your data! There is still some peace of mind in keeping your personal life and your business life "offline."

I've often thought about going paperless, and it's not as easy as it sounds. It's certainly not an overnight process either—there are a lot of factors to consider. It takes time to fully understand the ramifications and implications of leaving the "papered" world behind, and if you're years into your small business, you might prefer to avoid the thought of a paper-free workplace. In any case, there isn't a clear-cut answer for every business, and ultimately the choice is yours to make. Do your research so you can decide for yourself if the pros outweigh the challenges.

Legal & Ethical Issues

Legal issues and business ethics are a broad-spectrum topic and should ultimately be handled by your lawyer. But typically, these topics fall into a few categories:

- Avoid breaking the criminal law in your business activities.
- Avoid action against your customers that might result in civil lawsuit.
- Avoid anything that is bad for the company's image.

Why is this important? The result of any of these three things more or less will cost you business money and will diminish your business reputation. At startup, you will rely on your personal morals to conduct your business. Once you begin to grow and add employees, your task will be to carry these same business morals into the spirit of the company and lead by example.

The fact is that being moral and ethical in business is costly. It's costly to provide a safe and environmentally friendly workplace. Truthful advertising and humane working conditions are other examples. It can be all too tempting for you as a business owner to cut corners on ethical practices, but when you do, you run the risk of being called out by your customers or employees.

However, you can have an ethical, profitable business. It's about doing the right thing and proving that you're a trustworthy business. As you lie down at night and think about your day's activities, are you worried about your actions of that day? Make it a point to fall asleep soundly and without worry. Do the right thing and treat your customers and your employees right.

09

Marketing Your Business

In all honesty, marketing has to be my favorite part of owning my own business. This is my chance to show my individuality and to be creative. When I market my business, I have a chance to show what sets my company apart from the others in the industry. This is the time and place to show the customer that a trusted, well-meaning service provider is out there ready to take on their business with honesty and a work ethic. When I am searching for a product or service, these are the things I look for. It only seems smart to convey these same attributes to my customers.

Part of my daily routine is taking time to sniff out the competition. What services do they provide exactly? What offers are they making to the public? What advertising techniques are they using? I then assess my own business, asking these same questions. Imitation is the sincerest form of flattery, and that goes both ways. No one wants to copy the competition, but sometimes it can't be helped. If I am offering a service or a perk that makes me successful, others will want to jump on the bandwagon. Watching the competition helps me to stay ahead of the curve and remain on top in this industry.

In this day and age, marketing has many different forms. If you aren't savvy with Twitter, Facebook, blogging, Google, etc., you need to read up and get in the know. Identify the ways the customer is searching for reliable service providers and find a way to get the name of your business on those lists. That is the heart of marketing and the best way to become successful and grow.

Think outside the box and get as creative as you can. That is the name of the game. Find a way to make your business stand out and become a household name. If the name of your business is what first pops into the heads of customers when they are trying to decide how to fix the pickle they have found themselves in, then you know that all of your hard work and great marketing strategies have paid off.

Get moving and get your name out there . . .

Assess the Competition

First and foremost, before you start any marketing plan you're going to want to find out whom you are competing against and how they are advertising. You might even find that there are some giants out there that have huge marketing budgets, which may seem intimidating. If your goal is to take over the "big boys" market, then you have quite a task ahead of you and your goals may not be realistic at this time. The simple answer is not to market in the same way that big business advertises, and quite frankly you probably wouldn't be able to manage this financially anyway.

I've often wondered how small businesses make it. There's a lot of discussion about how Walmart is killing the "mom-and-pop" hardware stores and grocery stores around the country. While some of this may be true, and if you're a small "mom-and-pop" trying to compete directly with Walmart, it will be a tough road. The solution is to get creative and make sure to offer services and specials that differentiate your business from the big guys. Once you figure out that your local "big box" company is offering computer repair services, it's time to find out exactly what they are offering and at what pricing. You will want this for your analysis, and it might even become part of your marketing plan as well.

Next you'll move to the medium- and small-business market—businesses that most likely have marketing budgets similar to your own. The best way to do this is via

What Is a Search Engine?

A search engine is a webpage or service that allows you to actively search the Internet with a keyword or keywords of your choosing. The resulting pages that are displayed after a search is submitted are called the results pages. The results on these pages are delivered by the search engine assuming some factors about you, your location, and/or your prior searching habits. The best known and most frequently used search engine is www.google.com, but each has its own algorithm and may display different results on a particular keyword search.

the Internet. Since you're a computer repair business, you had better be conversant with the Internet and use its resources to your advantage.

The Internet can tell you an awful lot about your competition. You'll have a website and so will your competitors. This gives you twenty-four-hour access to learn about the guys across the tracks and find out what they are saying, offering, or doing on their site—and decide whether you need to match or beat what they are offering.

Today there are a number of tools, resources, and services for getting insights into competitors' traffic data. When beginning your online competition search, you may opt to pay for this service for a nominal cost.

When deciding which service to use, you'll want to find the service that can provide the most for the money and weigh the pros and cons of each. While I am not an expert in this field, I personally have had luck using www.alexa.com and www.compete.com when looking for general traffic statistics for competitors' websites. Compete.com is interesting because it's entirely devoted to helping businesses analyze their competition.

Once you decipher who might be your biggest competition on the Internet you'll want to get to know their websites. Most certainly your ideas will be amazing and cutting edge, but don't discount the competition; the established businesses in your field will have some great ideas too that you can capitalize on!

I would caution you to use your competitors' websites only as guidelines for your business. You don't want to go and scrape off the text or pictures and use them on your site. This will just end up in a lawsuit against you for copyright infringement,

What's the Competiton Doing?

I've paid consultants to assess the competition. There are many search engine optimization (SEO) companies out there, and they can do a phenomenal job of finding out what your competition is doing on the Internet. I've received full reports on how many pages each of my main competitor sites have (depth) plus how many clicks they are each receiving (reach).

It really depends on how detailed and how interested you are in finding out what your competitors are doing. As a small start-up, you may not have this option, but as you grow this information can be extremely helpful and give you an edge.

trademark infringement, or worse. You're going to want your website to be unique and yours, not a copy of someone else's hard work.

Imitation Is the Sincerest Form of Flattery—Sometimes

It was a Monday morning, and we received a call from a customer who was complaining that a repair we completed was not done properly. Since this can happen from time to time, we tried to help the customer over the phone initially, per our company policy, to see if we could resolve the issue.

So the first thing we do is look up the customer record in our database. This gives us the proper customer information, such as type of device repaired, when it was repaired, and what was completed. However, in this case, my customer service representative could not locate the customer record in our system.

This caused the customer to become angry. There was a bit of a heated conversation with my customer service representative, who felt very uneasy and helpless. Without being able to locate the "proof" that the customer had even used us in the past, it was very difficult to provide service or support for the issue. The customer then asked to speak to the owner.

I picked up the call and calmly tried to assist the customer. I assured the customer that my representative was only doing her job and that without an order number or the ability to find the order in our system, it was a bit of an odd situation.

I then played detective and said, "Most of our customers get our telephone number off of their repair invoice—would you mind telling me where you got our telephone number this morning?"

The customer replied, "It's on your website; I'm looking at it right now."

Knowing very well that our telephone number is posted on every page of our site, I asked, "What website are you looking at?"

This is when the mystery was solved. The customer gave me a competitor's website. However, under the "Support" section of their website was all of the support information from my website, copied and pasted verbatim into the competitor's site, including our telephone number and the instruction to call us for support. The competitor was in such a hurry to paste some information onto their site that they forgot to replace the support telephone number with their own.

So I called my lawyer and within one day the competitor removed the copyrighted material and wrote their own copy.

What happened to the customer? I took care of the issue. I picked up the unit from the customer, performed the repair properly, and sent it back, all at no charge. I landed a new customer for life that day.

Why Your Services Provide Value

Think of it from the perspective of your customers . . . why should they choose your business for service? When you're developing your business, keep in mind that you want to be a difference maker, someone who stands out among the crowd of other entrepreneurs in your field. Doing the same thing that the guy down the street is doing won't impress your customers. Doing the same thing that the guy down the street is doing with added value does impress and ultimately lands more business on your doorstep.

This is where you need to decide to make your mark. I decided to make my mark by offering twenty-four-hour turnaround on all of my repairs, and I stuck with it. Since there was virtually no one else in the industry offering this type of service, I felt that it was just the marketing punch I needed. You will want to come up with your own "difference maker" as well.

You're thinking about starting a business and you have an idea that will fill a void in the current marketplace. There is a need in the marketplace for computer repair—this is a given. When I started Mission Repair, I looked at the existing repair market on the Internet and saw extremely limited options for customers. Unless you didn't mind paying exorbitantly high prices and waiting two weeks or more for your computer repairs to be done, you were just out of luck. Yikes! And moreover bad reviews and testimonials could have filled volumes on each business. I wanted to do something very different because I cared and because I saw the opportunity to build a meaningful business.

That was our market entry: to provide necessary services (filling a need) at real-world prices in an honest, fair, and prompt manner. We thought outside the "repair box" and pioneered the twenty-four-hour repair with overnight shipping to and from the customer's location. No one else was doing this properly, and we seized the market void.

But then came the competition—if your idea catches on, you can bet that others will follow. This is when differentiation between your brand and everyone else's becomes incredibly important. It's almost never enough that you were first. You have to be the best, and it is a constant race. I'm proud to say that Mission Repair continues to win this race, but it isn't easy. And remember, it's a marathon, not a sprint. On the following page are the top three tips for how to distinguish yourself from the ever-fluctuating pool of competitors.

Be Memorable

I was once visited by a salesman who was trying to sell packaging to me. You know, shipping materials, tape, boxes, and other common warehouse items. It's tough to make a difference in the packaging market, and it's hard to stand out. If you're like me, the door-to-door salesman who "cold calls" his customers can get tiring and even annoying. I felt that if I wanted packaging, I'd call him when I was ready.

Well, this guy was pleasant, had decent prices, and never pushed too hard. But he also left doughnuts. He would come around about once a month, leaving me a new price list, with some fresh doughnuts.

After several trips in to see me and without an order placed by me, he left doughnuts again.

Several months went by and he never faltered. I was finally in a place to start business with this guy, and he was right there for me. He wasn't the cheapest vendor in the market, but the relationship he developed with me by stopping in to say hi and bring me breakfast every few weeks showed me that he was willing to work and work hard for me.

Ten years have passed since my first visit from him, and to this day he's my packaging salesperson. In fact, we are dear friends now, and he's got my business for life.

Doughnuts were his difference maker.

Choose Your Core Values & Implement Them Better Than Anyone Else

At your business, make your customer the priority. Always. For me, this not only means using the best possible parts but it also means admitting mistakes and fixing them. When customers choose your service, they know that they will be treated honestly and fairly.

Innovate

As soon as you establish your methods and set a standard, there is no time to sit back and enjoy the ride. You have to keep moving on to what's next, always creating the next great service, warranty, or feature that no one else has thought of. One of the ways we have done this is by growing our service line as technology has grown. So you may start out servicing Windows-based computers, but you need to be flexible and continue to expand your lines. My son Casey helps to inspire my constant innovation. All I need to do is watch what new electronic gadget he's into, and then try to provide services for it.

Be Patient

Yes, when you're starting a business this is hard to do, but if you are working too fast, you're not giving your hard-built brand a chance. You must maintain the integrity of every service and guarantee you offer, to keep your customer's trust and continued loyalty in the future.

Marketing 101

As you launch your new small business, you should focus heavily on a complete and accurate website and your ability to conduct e-commerce, which we will discuss further in chapter 10. There are many components to e-commerce, but to start you will need the following:

- A product or a service
- A place to sell the product or service—in e-commerce, a website displays the products in some way and acts as the place
- A way to get people to come to your website
- A way to accept orders—typically an online form of some sort
- A way to accept money—normally a merchant account taking credit-card payments. This piece requires a secure ordering page and a connection to

a bank. Or you may use more traditional billing techniques either online or through the mail.

- A fulfillment facility to ship packages to customers
- A way to accept returns
- A way to handle warranty claims if necessary
- A way to provide customer service (often through e-mail, online forms, online knowledge bases, FAQs, etc.)

Visiting your website only to follow links that land on an "under construction" page will lead your customers away from your store and into the hands of the competition. Whether you build your webpage yourself or contract it to a website consultant, you must insist that your site be ready for opening day. Don't trust yourself to "get back to it" or feel that "it doesn't matter." Since your website must be complete and ready for business, it should be your primary focus as your first marketing tool and your best salesperson. Just think about it . . . a good website will take orders for you twenty-four hours per day. It does not need to be built as a nationwide service site and if you only want to service customers in your hometown, you're still going to want to have a site on the web.

Lesson 1: Make Your Website Visible to the Public

When thinking in terms of my business and how I want my customers to find me, I use the Internet from my customers' point of view. I will go to a search engine and type in a phrase (otherwise known as a keyword) and scour the results. Give this a try for yourself. Since you're moving into the computer repair business, try searching for the keyword "computer repair." You're going to find hundreds of businesses from all over the country that work very hard to get their search results on this front page. This is known as SEO (search engine optimization, see page 166) and is something you're going to want to know a little bit about. The key is to fine-tune your search query and to remember to think like your customer. Maybe your new business is in Boulder, Colorado. When you perform your search on the Internet, use the keyword "Boulder Computer Repair" to see a narrower list of results and your true local competitors. Then type in "Boulder Computer Service" and see yet another list of websites. Finally try something obscure and relevant to your business. Maybe you're planning on servicing Dell computers. Now search for "Boulder Dell Inspiron Screen Repair" and you will most likely find an even different set of websites, some of which might not even be relevant to that keyword right on the front page. Now that's the kind of keyword you want to focus on in your SEO efforts—because the more services you can have land on the first page of your search engine, the more people are going to see your website. The more people you get on your website, the more opportunities you'll have to convert them into customers.

Lesson 2: Make Your Website Your Best Salesperson

Since your website should be a large part of your marketing plan, you want to be as cohesive and intuitive as possible. Far too often when I search the web for a product or service, I am turned off by my shopping experience on a particular site so I move on to another.

When you develop your site, this is your brand and initially the entire face of your company. Additionally, a nice-looking website is one thing, but an informative and working website is another. Don't lose sales because of a broken link or inaccurate text. Instead, walk through your own website from the viewpoint of your customer. Have a family member act as a customer and place a test order. This will simply help point out the flaws, glitches, and weaknesses before you go to market. From a customer standpoint, it will be an easy decision—if a computer repair company's website isn't 100 percent, how can the service be? Remember you're the expert in their eyes on all things technical, so your website had better be on the mark!

Lesson 3: Expand Your Reach

So you've got your website running, you're taking some orders, and the information you're presenting on the Internet is accurate. That's a great step in getting your brand out to your local market.

When you're ready to expand your reach, you can do so on any level that you choose. Lots of things are possible. But you can never know what is truly possible for your business unless you make an all-out effort. And you can't make an all-out effort unless you step away from business as usual; look at the big picture and objectively assess what will take you to the next level.

Say you have your business off the ground and you're offering repairs on Macintosh computers. Maybe you describe your business this way: "We provide top-of-the-line service and repair experiences with outstanding support for discriminating Apple customers . . ."

Sounds good, but what do you really do?

Keep Your Eye on the Prize

I started my business on a kitchen table. I bet on myself and told my family that this was going to work, so I made it work. I didn't have a huge pile of money to get things started, so I spent all of my time perfecting my website. Within six months, I needed to hire my first employee.

This is where the game changed a bit. I decided that I wanted a small business, but how small . . . or how big? I figured that I'd let the market take me there and I would just add employees, as I needed.

I ran a tight ship and my motto was "If I can't afford it, I can't do it." It was a blessing that I didn't get a bank loan or take money from a private investor. The blessing was that I didn't owe anyone money for anything.

So I expanded my reach. Instead of solely offering services to local customers, I worked with FedEx to get some excellent shipping rates, then offered my services to the nation.

What happened next? I started getting in devices from California, from Texas, from New York, and then I hired a couple of technicians to help me, plus a shipping/receiving clerk. The phone started ringing off the hook, so I hired a couple of customer service representatives. I was expanding at a good pace, manageable enough for me to not lose sight of my core values and promises that I was making to my customers.

I was then able to increase my marketing budget and I hired a firm to help me optimize my website. This increased my rankings on the Internet and made my site more visible to even more customers. I was quickly becoming an expert on all things "computer repair" and other sites were referring to my website because it contained a lot of good information.

I focused on blogging, which has a worldwide reach and a connection to my website. Do you see the benefits here? Authoring a blog that provided "read-worthy" material and that linked to my website was like having another voice on the Internet speaking to a large group of people.

I was then able to dive into television advertising and I even ran a Super Bowl commercial (actually two Super Bowl commercials in the same game) with the help of a production company. Boy was I nervous the day of the Super Bowl!

> I went from hungry guy at the kitchen table to blog-writing author to employer to the Super Bowl to authoring this book. How does something like this happen? I must have had some professional help, right?
>
> No, it all started with the will to get my brand right. I typed a lot in the beginning, on my website and blog, kept my promises to my customers and provided services of value. I do not have a college degree in business, nor did I have any idea about employee taxes, advertising, or blogging. I didn't have any idea about these things until I did them. I expanded my reach, kept control of my ideals, and enjoyed natural business and immense personal growth.

To turn a profit, every month you need to sell x number of services, perform y number of repairs, and invoice z number of customers. That's your business: sell, repair, and collect payment. Without the right combination of x, y, and z, you don't have a business.

Because selling services naturally leads to repairs and then to invoicing customers, just selling more services automatically drives need for labor and repairs and ultimately more money coming in the door, which gives you the ability to expand your reach.

So pick a week—or better yet, a month—to focus primarily on sales. Turn yourself, and your employees if you have them, into cold callers and appointment setters. Reconnect with old customers and friends who might have a fit with your business. Increase direct-response advertising spending; forget "branding" and focus on marketing efforts that directly generate leads, appointments, and sales.

Do what it takes to double or even triple your average number of sales calls. What could happen if your business went all out to determine its true top speed in terms of sales? I know that when I drive my employees, lead by example, and truly work off-the-charts hard, we are all in a better position for growth.

Sales are just an example. Maybe productivity is the key driver in your business. Maybe quality is more important than productivity. Decide what you really do, and hold your throttle wide open and find out what is truly possible for your business. Sound impossible? Then pick something small and knock that out. Go hard for a day or a week; you'll go home surprised by what you managed to achieve, and you'll be eager for more. It's the entrepreneurial spirit that should drive you.

After all, if you're not willing to work hard, it will be a long, tough road. But if you're determined to be successful, work smart and expand your reach. It will pay off.

Networking

In the beginning, it will be an excellent idea to reach out and meet other people in your business or just meet other business owners in your area. Start with your local chamber of commerce.

Most chambers put on weekly or monthly meetings that are free to attendees. This is an excellent way to get out of the home office and in front of live potential customers. In fact, these types of gatherings can bring untold new leads and sales that you might not have ever received otherwise. I've been to countless chamber meetings and it's a great way to get yourself in front of a group of other like-minded people. Yes, as you meet people you will listen to what they have to offer and you should accept that as part of your business education. Maybe there's a potential partnership or other business offering that will benefit you along the way.

Additionally, there are networking websites that offer entrepreneurs a chance to ask each other questions, run ideas by one another, and offer ideas. Set up business accounts on Facebook.com, Linkedin.com, and Twitter.com to offer direct means of communication with you. You want to be seen and heard, so using social sites is an excellent means of networking.

Social-Media Marketing

Social-media marketing is the new kid on the block, but it is packing a powerful punch. It's where things can go "viral." Viral means becoming very popular in a very short amount of time. If you're an Internet marketer (and I sure hope that you will become one!), then you want everyone in the world to see your latest innovation, so "viral" is a word you should love.

Today, "going viral" refers to the sharing of something on the Internet like a website or a video, via e-mail or a social website such as Facebook or Twitter. Viral subject matter can consist of just about anything. Very funny videos can go viral and have thousands and even millions of views in a matter of days. Catching something unique, funny, or even scary on film can cause a video to be shared and seen. The common characteristic of viral videos is that they are interesting and they inspire people to share them with their friends. Viral videos started circulating via e-mail long before video sites like YouTube were ever around. There are many contenders for the first "viral" video in history, so there's some controversy as to which video might have earned the initial honors.

"David After Dentist," posted on YouTube in 2009, is a great example of a video that can be dubbed "viral." It has had over one hundred million views, and is a simple, funny video about a child who is recovering from anesthesia, posted by his father. The point is that while you may not know at the time that something you're recording will go viral, the idea of one hundred million views of a video that you produce should make you salivate.

The popularity of social-media sites is undeniable and they are here to stay. For each of these sites, you should immediately register a user name (and tie it to your business name), as it will be inevitable that you'll be reading Twitter and hitting the "Like" button on Facebook as a representative of your new venture.

Facebook

I'm sure that you've at least heard about Facebook. It doesn't matter if you're a grand-parent or a kindergartner, it's come up sometime in your presence in the last year. If you didn't understand what it was, that's OK, but you're going to want to get to know this little marketing gem of a website, and it can be absolutely free.

There's a lot of talk about "Liking" and "Likes" on Facebook, and for the entrepreneur this is the heart of the issue.

First, Facebook is a "social" site in that you can connect your Facebook page with a friend's page. Keep adding friends, and you build your friend list. There are some Facebook users who are merely friend "collectors" and the user with the most friends "wins." While this is an intriguing and frankly addicting goal, it seems that I know only about thirty people in my immediate world but I have over three hundred "friends" on my Facebook page. Facebook considers a "friend" anyone who accepts an invitation from a user.

It's a good idea to start a Facebook business page, separate from your personal page, that is solely dedicated to your business and what you can offer. This is a smart idea because you will garner friends from all walks of life on your business page who might not necessarily be interested in your personal habits. Also, Facebook does not allow you to run a business from your personal page.

Nevertheless, all of these connections make a huge network of people, a long chain from one Facebook page to the next that connects millions of pages to one another. Let's say I post an interesting link on my Facebook page that one of my friends passes on to his Facebook page. Then one of his friends (whom I don't know) likes the link and passes it on to his Facebook page. There's an interesting chain of postings that all derived from your profile. If you're in business for yourself, why not post some interesting business information, like a sale or giveaway?

It will be spread through the Facebook world, and the idea is to have this large network of people at your fingertips, then drive them back to your profile page, and then to your website to make a sale at your business. Is there something wrong with this picture? Absolutely not. As you do so, you'll also gain friend "invitations" that will grow your immediate network of "friends" and therefore add to the first level of exposure for you and your business.

YouTube

There's a brave new world out there in the marketing field and it's all about video. YouTube is quickly becoming as widely used as any other website on the Internet. Why? Because you can find a video of just about anything that you're looking for because most likely someone (like you) has recorded it and posted it.

I'm not going to beat around the bush—there is a lot of junk video on YouTube, but if you can sift through the rubble and get to the video that you want to see, it can be an invaluable source of information.

The nice part about YouTube is that you can "monetize" your videos. Monetize, as in "money." You can make money by allowing others to advertise just before, or within (as an overlay), your posted videos. This works well when you have a video that is producing a lot of views. There are entrepreneurs out there making some amazing videos and living solely off the monetization of their videos. Intrigued? Make yourself some money!

The problem lies in the fact that a junk video will not make you any money. This is where living and thinking like your customer will come in handy. As you progress in your business adventure, think about making an instructional "how-to" video for something that you service. I would be willing to bet that there are plenty of people who want to see a video on your very subject. When your customer sees a well-made video, sees a link to your website or even you in the video wearing a T-shirt that has your telephone number across the front, you will get business from the exposure.

Additionally, YouTube is a free website, and you cannot beat free. Once you get your free video posted, try pasting a link onto your Facebook profile page and watch the views add up!

LinkedIn

LinkedIn is a professional website and is touted as the world's largest professional network with over one hundred seventy-five million members, and growing rapidly. LinkedIn connects you to your trusted business contacts and helps you exchange ideas, thoughts, and opportunities with a broad range of professionals. In fact, I have a friend who had a clean and well-maintained LinkedIn page, was called by Apple, Inc., and was offered a full-time permanent position in Cupertino, California. He wasn't looking for a job, but his LinkedIn page did the work for him and landed him a fantastic position in his field of expertise.

Twitter

Twitter is a site that I just didn't believe in at first, but if you see me now, I'm an active Twitter contributor.

For anyone who is trying to stay connected via the social networks, Twitter should not be neglected. If you are new to this media application, you will discover that you can change the way you communicate with others in one hundred and forty characters or less. It's important to remember that when using this social-media site, it can become quite addicting.

1. Twitter is simple to use. There are many apps for Twitter, which makes posting from your smartphone an easy task.
2. You can follow some interesting people. There are a lot of important and relevant people on Twitter, and you can read what they are doing via a "feed." Be interactive with these people, and they will follow your posts on Twitter. When you have people following you, that's a good thing!
3. You can interact with your customers. It's true—some of your customers may prefer to communicate via Twitter, so this means that you're going to want to embrace it.

Now link your Twitter account with your Facebook account, and when you post a new tweet, it will also post to your Facebook page. That's being social, active, and current . . . and that's the key to these social-media sites.

Traditional Marketing Ideas

You know all about traditional marketing ideas—they are the marketing ideas that we grew up with. Before the Internet, there was a standard for marketing that can still work today. The key is to pay the right price for the traditional marketing piece. Although it may seem that traditional marketing is dead, that's simply not true.

Newspapers

There are still some newspapers making profits firing up the printing presses each night and hand-delivering stacks of papers all over town. Advertising rates have fallen, and you can find the right deals. You may be able to negotiate a great rate on flyer inserts, so you can have full-color ads that might make a better impression than the standard black-and-white ads we saw as kids.

Most print newspapers have online versions too, so you can capitalize on a single price for both versions if you negotiate right. Remember that nowadays more people read newspapers online than in print, but you don't want to exclude those diehard paper readers from knowing about you and your services.

Direct-Mail Programs

This is an interesting marketing program that can yield great success. There are programs offered by the United States Postal Service and other third parties that can deliver your full-color flyers to geographic regions of your choosing, for a low price per flyer. Low cost as in about a 75 percent savings over sending a single letter to a friend.

The direct-mail approach works by setting up a region with the mail carrier, and regardless of the name of the household, the carrier will insert one of your special flyers into each mailbox, in that region. Since the mail carrier doesn't need to worry whether the right person gets your flyer or not (because they will all get it) the price is far less expensive per piece to deliver the flyers to each house.

This can work if the flyer is right. Look at your own habits though. When you open your mailbox look at the "junk mail" (and bear in mind that your flyer will be considered junk mail) and see what appeals to you and what doesn't. My guess is that if you're like me, you don't need to see another carpet-cleaning flyer at the moment, so you toss those in the garbage. However, an iPod repair business offering specials on battery replacements while I wait? That might work because my iPod needs a new battery. You never know.

Magazines

Print magazines are still being produced and distributed. Like newspapers, print magazines will probably have digital "e-zine" versions as well, which basically gives you double the exposure for one price. Print magazines used to be a very expensive way to advertise, but these days the prices are low so don't rule out the possibility!

Trade Shows

Trade shows in your niche can be valuable networking tools and an easy way to gather customers in a large group. It's a way to represent your business live and in person and make personal connections that can be remembered. There is a spirit of networking and camaraderie built into a lot of these events, so they are well worth attending.

Can't find a trade show in your area or even in your niche? Try looking locally for "Think Green" trade shows. You can rent a booth and boast that you're saving the landfills by "repairing rather than disposing." You'll fit right into a show that may be attended by tens of thousands of potential customers, with very little or no competition for you.

Yellow Pages

Yellow what? Remember "Let your fingers do the walking"? I personally don't use the Yellow Pages anymore, and I haven't received a copy on my doorstep since I canceled the telephone land-line at my house, but the Yellow Pages are still in print and are still in use. Once again, if you're looking for some exposure, think about your target audience and make wise decisions.

Think about this: Your customer has a broken computer and can't get online to find you, so he pulls out his next option and reverts to the phone book. He looks up "Computer Repair" and there's your ad, begging him to call you. It's an option that is completely feasible and may garner you some sales, but the price has to be right!

Nontraditional & Unique Marketing Ideas

As you continue to ponder how you are going to get more customers, try to think outside the box. The goal here is to find an easy way to reach more customers and not pay a premium to compete in the same space as your competitors.

Have you ever seen a kid on a street corner with a sandwich board or holding a sign dancing and directing people into the "We Buy Gold" store? This marketing concept, which dates back to the 19th century, has always seemed to work. If it didn't work, these guys would be gone. This is a great example of another nontraditional marketing technique that can drive customers to your location without a lot of expense.

My New Company Uniform

After scratching my head thinking "I can't afford to pay for all of this marketing," I needed a new idea. I was out with a friend and I overheard someone at a restaurant saying how she dropped her iPhone and was at a loss as to where or how to have it repaired. Naturally, I apologized and interjected that I couldn't help but overhear the conversation and handed her my card. Of course, I could fix iPhones and this was a potential new customer!

The next day, I got a call from my lead and repaired her iPhone. This gave me a new idea, and I had a few T-shirts made. Very simply, the front of the shirt said, "I fix iPhones." On the back, it had my website and telephone number.

A short time later my wife and I were on vacation in Vail, Colorado, and we both happened to be wearing our shirts at a bar and grill while sitting on the patio chatting.

Without notice, a gentleman came up to us, set his cracked iPhone on the table in front of me, and said simply, "Help me."

Had I not been wearing my new favorite shirt, I would not have reached this customer. Well, maybe it was my wife wearing the shirt that got his attention as she is far better to look at than I am, but we will chalk it up to the T-shirt making the sale!

Another way to bring business is to find a theme and enter your business into parades. Just think about it . . . many city parades offer an immediate connection to thousands of potential customers.

Guerrilla Marketing

You can also take your nontraditional marketing ideas to a guerrilla marketing firm, or even run a guerrilla marketing campaign ad or event on your own. Guerrilla marketing is an advertising strategy that focuses on low-cost, unconventional marketing tactics that yield maximum results at a local or regional level.

Guerrilla marketing may be the right solution for your small business. When executed well, its low-cost and highly targeted format pays off. It's a way to get noticed and differentiated from the competition while earning a reputation for being cutting edge and different.

Guerrilla marketing is a broad term, and entering a parade is a simple guerrilla marketing idea. However, for many the term signifies a "shocking" form of advertising, and some say that if it's not "newsworthy," it's not guerrilla marketing. While traditional media can be useful for advertising and marketing, the cost can be high. Small businesses can opt to use the media in more of a newsworthy and journalistic way by organizing and hosting events that the media will cover for free as a routine part of local news coverage. For example, a small business can host a car wash and donate the money to charity. Guerrilla marketing methods such as this work when all employees wear clothing clearly showing the name, contact information, and web address of the company hosting the event.

A more "shocking" example would be to skydive while offering a promotion on

Everyone Loves a Parade

I was looking for other ways to get local business. I wanted my customers to know that I was right in their neighborhood, and since I didn't have a retail location they would never find us unless we told them about us. Once again I put my innovating cap on and thought "parades!"

We have several parades in our area each year. There are St. Patrick's Day parades, festival parades, city parades, Fourth of July parades . . . well, you get the idea. In fact, there are an amazing number of parades that I never even knew about. What was I going to enter? If you are going to be in a parade, you need to have a theme or a float of some kind, so I went into innovation mode.

I ended up doing some research on old military vehicles and purchased a restored 1968 M35A2, otherwise known as a Deuce and a Half or military transport. My business name is "Mission Repair," so I took the theme on a Mission with this military truck.

I had a couple of banners made, added some flags on the back, and entered every parade I could get in to. I asked for volunteers to help me as I drove this beast in and around our city to advertise my business. Guess what? It worked. People love the fact that it's a restored piece of history, and it appeals to a lot of people when I drive it. I still own this transport, and every year tens of thousands of people see it with my business name, website, and telephone number along the side as we rock the parade scene.

Nontraditional marketing works.

your business or a percentage off of your services for every 1,000 feet you fall. Donate a percentage to charity and have a custom parachute made with your logo on it. This particular stunt may be an exorbitantly expensive and risky proposition for a new business; however, it would certainly gain some attention!

I suggest as you perform your first guerrilla marketing advertisement, be patient. Then come up with another ad. As you continue to impress, customers will remember you. These techniques can work well if you have the courage.

Pay-Per-Click

Another fantastic way to bring people to your website is to use Google's "Pay-Per-Click" advertising. In fact, it can bring immediate sales and most certainly bring new customers to your website every day that you run your ads. This is a service that gets you on the front page of the Google search in which you advertise. Try a Google search of your own and take a look at these sponsored links, which typically show up as the top three results and along the right-hand side of the page.

For example, let's say that you want to offer Dell laptop keyboard repairs. Within the account that you open for your Google AdWords, you can set up a pay-per-click campaign titled "Dell Repairs," and then within that campaign you'd set up the key-words "Dell Laptop Keyboard Repairs." Google will then report back to you how much other businesses are paying for that word combination. The more you pay, the higher you'll land on the list of advertisers.

So you understand this more, the account team at Google will be happy to assist. Additionally scores of Google-trained businesses will evaluate and manage your pay-per-click campaigns for a fee; in the long run it may be worth the expense.

Google isn't the only pay-per-click option out there. Facebook.com, Bing.com, Yahoo.com, and even Bidadvertiser.com offer plans to meet any budget.

Blogging, Blogging, Blogging

Blogging. This was a foreign word to me several years ago. I felt that I was "above" blogging and imagining myself sitting behind a computer typing stories to my readers just didn't seem like an effective way for me to spend my time.

A blog is short for "web log," but the exact definition is still very much in flux. It's original and basic purpose is that it's literally an online diary or journal that can contain photos, movie clips, and links to other websites. These journal entries are made by the author, otherwise known as the "blogger."

A typical blog, when created, starts at the top on the page while yesterday's news scrolls down the page. The oldest blog entries hence are at the bottom of the page or several pages back, depending on how long the blogger has been writing.

Most blogs allow the reader to leave comments, and these comments can be moderated by the blog administrator or the blogger. Typically this interactive nature also allows readers to link to other blogs and therefore "network" and interact with your entries. This can also be called interacting within the "blogosphere," in which several blogs with a common subject or interest are linked to one another. The blogosphere is important because it keeps people interested in what your blog might have to say.

The blogosphere may not happen on its own. You, as the blogger, will need to read other blogs, comment on them, link to your blog, and start the networking process in many cases. If your goal is to use your blog as a marketing tool, then this will be necessary. Of course the web is a crowded field, and many of the millions of blogs out there are not worth reading. However, there are thousands of active bloggers who have the same mentality, passion, and drive as you do, so networking with them is a good thing and may in fact teach you something.

To get started on a blog, you need to use a service (which can be free) to get going. I have used Wordpress.com and Blogger.com in the past, but if you do a simple search in Google for "how to start a blog," you will see several guides, discussions, articles, and even blog entries that will help you get rolling.

Essentially, you'll need to come up with a blog concept. In your case, it may simply be "the life of a computer repair technician," but I prefer a title that might catch a reader's interest, like "Joe's Repair Tips—How to Save Bundle on Computer Repair." Either of these titles and topics is engaging, but the title and theme of your blog will initially attract readers and keep it interesting!

Remember that a blog is something that you are passionate about—and since you're imagining that you're in business for yourself as you read this, your passion will be your business. It's great to speak about your business, the trials, the growth, and the new services that you might offer all in your blog. It's a personal perspective and can garner new customers just from their perception of you.

I tend to write blogs on a daily (the best option) or weekly basis. Within my repair blog, I have posts that are purely personal. Then I have posts that are purely business. I will then mix the two and have blog entries that start on a personal topic but then move to business. In all cases, I try to remember that my blog was designed as a marketing tool, so I try to make my entries appeal to everyone. I never talk about politics, religion, or anything of a subjective nature because my blog is marketing—and I don't want to drive away a prospective customer with a potentially controversial opinion. If you want a blog to talk about politics, then start a blog that talks about politics. My advice is to keep these argumentative topics out of your business arena!

If your blog topics are engaging, you will find that some posts that you never expected others to read will garner a lot of attention. Other "masterpieces" will sit stagnant. This is the beauty of a blog though—as you keep writing you will hit on likable topics that will bring people to your blog, and since this is a marketing tool, they will pay attention and click a link to your website. That's the magic of blogging.

Some Blogs Are Worth the Time

So back in 2010 I was busy writing my blog and it was going well. I gathered several loyal readers and found out that staying on top of my blog and the comments left within proved to readers that I was attentive and communicative. I always worked in a line or two about "business" in each post. It happened that we stumbled upon a part for a tablet and in fact it was the internal frame to the very first Apple iPad. Since the first iPad had not been released at that time and there was much speculation about the iPad, its size, what it would do, if it would have a camera, and how consumers would use it, I felt that the frame would be a good blog topic.

Here's that blog posting (notice its simplicity, with two pictures added):

Hello all,

We received our first shipment of iPad parts today. Here's one of the metal internal frames:
Upon opening them up and getting our hands on some of these rare items, we immediately noticed what appears to be a "spot" for a camera within the iPad frame.
Hmmmm.

We pulled a camera from a Unibody MacBook. Just a standard camera unit that we see every day.

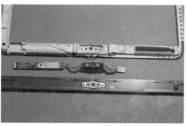

Guess what, it fits right in there. The camera slips in the frame, the lens fits in the hole, the LED that indicates that the camera is on fits, and the ambient light sensor hole is also correct. It appears that the plans to have a camera in the iPad is a reality.

I'm looking forward to the iPad . . . when the next generation is released! More inside pics coming soon!

— Ryan

This blog entry launched on February 22, 2010, and it made blog history. We had 31,205 individual readers of the blog the very first day. We additionally had over 10,000 readers on my "About Us" page of the blog, which then turned in to thousands of clicks over to my website (of course my "About Us" page has a link to my website!). After this posting I gained new prominence and respect as a valued and trusted site to visit. Who would have known that this blog would have gone viral? I never would have known if I hadn't written it.

Blogging ends up being a great way to point users (customers) to your website. There's a lot of gratification in writing a blog, and it's exciting when you add rich and relevant content to a new website and then wait for the search engines to find and promote it. When I say "promote it," I mean "index it" and put it within the search results of a user's query.

Indexing a site, even your blog, by the search engines will help your site rise to the top of the searches. The more relevant your blog, the more readers, and the more the blog conforms to the search engines' checklists, the quicker and higher it rises in the resulting search rankings.

If you're sitting and waiting for your site to be indexed and ranked, it can be a lot like watching grass grow. Just keep moving forward, and eventually you'll have to get out that lawnmower.

Publicity

At its core, publicity is the simple act of making a suggestion to the press or a reporter that leads to the inclusion of a company or product in a story. Newspapers, magazines, TV programs, and radio shows have large amounts of space to fill and they depend on publicists to help provide story ideas, interview subjects, background information, and other material.

I'm Not Bothered by Paparazzi

When I first started running TV commercials, I went big and bought a local Super Bowl spot to run in the Kansas City area. It was a bold move, and I remember many sleepless nights wondering if I was making the right decision.

The day came, and the Super Bowl ads ran. It was an exciting game, even though I can't remember what teams played that day. I was too focused on my new commercials, and the anticipation was incredible.

Well it worked—the next day we had a line at our doorstep. There was a wait in our lobby all day and most customers commented that they "didn't even know that we existed" until they saw our Super Bowl ads. I was relieved that it was taking hold and customers were happy to find us.

Within an hour, I received a call from a local TV news station that wanted to interview me as a small-business owner and run a story about a local "success." Within an hour we had a news team and a reporter in our service lab filming, and we were excited about our decision to risk the cost of the Super Bowl ad space to get new business.

I spent thirty minutes in front of the camera, nervous as could be, answering questions about my business for everyone to see. The story aired on TV several times that night, the day after the Super Bowl. The reporter gave me his card and said, "Call me if you ever have anything exciting that we should know about in the future." Oh yeah!

A week later, I was at the dentist for a routine cleaning. While sitting in the waiting room, a lady came up to me and said, "Hey, aren't you that computer guy I saw on TV?"

The publicity was working and for a moment I was almost famous. She didn't want my autograph, but she did take my business card. Publicity works, it's important, and you need to be ready for anything.

For the most part, the act of making a suggestion to reporters, if they think your lead is newsworthy, will lead to one of two types of coverage:

- A story created from scratch built around the story angle you suggest (i.e., a feature story on your company, a story about a big gamble on a Super Bowl commercial, a cutting-edge new program that you invent, etc.)
- The inclusion of your company or service in an already existing story (i.e., the reporter is already working on a story about your field, and your lead results in your being included in the piece).

Press Release

Another way to get the press's attention is to write a press release. Simply put, a press release is a news story (that you write) that presents the most newsworthy aspect of your company and services in a format and language familiar to a journalist. A good press release places the newsworthy angle at the very top (much like the lead paragraph of a well-written news story) and is free of hype and over-promotion. It's factual and interesting and needs to grab the reporter's attention within a line or two. Paragraphs subsequent to the lead may include background information, spokesperson quotations, and other information that can help put the newsworthiness of the story in perspective.

Press releases can be submitted through a press release service for a fee, with a plethora of vendors on the Internet available to assist.

Pitch Letter

You can also write a journalist directly, by submitting a pitch letter. While the press release is written in third person, the pitch letter allows for direct communication between you and the reporter. It's an opportunity to pique interest, form a relationship, and persuade. Bad pitch letters begin with boring formalities or promotional hype. Good pitch letters begin with a striking opening that immediately alerts the journalist to an interesting story possibility (e.g., if I'm promoting a new charitable program, "Mission Repair is donating 5 percent of all repair profits to local schools").

The pitch letter has one purpose: to persuade the journalist to read the attached press release. Personalize it, keep it short, personally sign it, clip it to the front of your press release, and mail it to your media outlets of choice. Try the TV stations.

Finding something newsworthy might get cumbersome, but you need to make it happen!

Press Releases Work Well

Here's an example of a successful press release that I wrote, which was read by over 2,400 newsrooms across the country within a matter of days:

The new iPad is amazing, but it has a fragile screen.

Mission Repair saves the day with their amazing services.

Mission Repair, a staple in the service industry for the last five years, is already seeing new iPads in for repair.

The screen is just as fragile as the first two versions and this service company has seen immediate demand from the market. Their business is based on amazing customer service and they have launched their new iPad screen repairs at just $210 installed, which is the best price on the Internet today.

New iPad screen-repair service. Cracked glass fixed in 24 hours!

They can have the customer's 4G LTE iPad picked up from anywhere in the USA, brought back to their service lab, have the unit repaired within 24 hours, and sent back overnight to the customer's location.

If a customer breaks an iPad, this is the place to go for service.

Mission Repair offers "Got Repair" benefits on many of their services. If you use Mission Repair and ever break or damage the part again, they will repair it again for a small service fee—no other business in the market offers this advantage! See the website for details.

About Mission Repair: The 2009, 2010, 2011, 2012, and 2013 Award Winning iPhone Repair Center. Mission Repair is your choice for full-service iPad, iPod, MacBook, and cell phone repair services. Mission Repair currently offers repair services for iPods, iPhones, Apple laptop computers (including MacBook Air, MacBook Pro, MacBook, PowerBook, and iBook), gaming consoles (including PSP), and cell phones with new programs coming online often.

Mission Repair is accredited though the Greater Kansas City Better Business Bureau and is a proud member of the Olathe, Kansas Chamber of Commerce. They employ Apple Certified Macintosh Technicians.

With a 100 percent customer service mentality, www.missionrepair.com is your one-stop repair service center with support for all makes and models of iPods, iPhones, and Macintosh portable systems, cell phones, and gaming consoles.

Mission Repair
19941 West 162nd Street
Olathe, Kansas 66062
(866) 638-8402
sales@missionrepair.com

To reporters who answer to the editor, a story is newsworthy if they feel that the audience will be interested in the topic. To uncover the newsworthiness of your business, think about your target customer. Put yourself in his or her shoes; in my case I want to appeal to customers who need service on items that I specialize in. What would make you excited, intrigued or interested? Now, think about how your business provides its services and meets the needs of potential customers.

Remember our pitch-letter opening for donating to schools? You might think that being one of several computer repair shops in your city might make it tough to be newsworthy, but "Mission Repair is donating 5 percent of all repair profits to local schools" should make a few business reporters stand up and take notice. In this case, the recent school cutbacks and closings were a hot topic. What gets them excited and intrigued? The notion that Mission Repair is giving money to schools to help ease the burden of budget cuts. What will interest them? The realization that there's a small business willing to do its part for the good of the community.

Notice that the pitch doesn't say, "Local business donates to charities" or "Ryan Arter, small business owner, has a rebate program on iPhone repairs." You want to pick an angle that may have some relevance to a local or even nationwide problem, and offer a solution.

The skill of coming up with angles for stories is a craft on its own, and while my example of donating to schools might not excite some reporters, it will catch the eye of others. And it did.

The fact is that reporters need stories. Remember that you're just the person to help them find those stories. It can be intimidating to call and speak to a reporter directly, but I've done it and it's worth the effort. I've even been given the invitation to call reporters when I see fit. Reporters are typically hurried and rushed, and they spend a lot of time answering phone calls from people wanting to pitch them all sorts of ridiculous stories. However, it's important to remember that they need you as much as you need them. If you are presenting a useful story idea professionally and courteously, you'll be surprised at how fast they will return to your business asking for more.

Other Advertising

Thinking about your customers and their demographic can be important when considering other forms of advertising.

A nifty way to make a big splash in advertising, especially if you're going to be providing on-site services, is to add a graphic to your vehicle. Most simply, you can have a car magnet made that is easily added when you're on a call or removed when you want your vehicle to be more personal. This is a good way to reach people when you're on the move and quite frankly if you're providing on-site services, your customers might feel more secure if you arrive in a company-labeled vehicle. It brings some legitimacy and security to your business.

Nothing Wrong with Bartering Some Ad Space

I wanted to try to run some ads in my local high school's monthly newspaper. I called the editor and asked her for some pricing, and as she listened to the scope of my business, she asked that I stop by her office.

Her department needed some help with a failing iPad, so I took it in and performed a repair. Afterward, she suggested that I run an ad and give a discount to students, or even better yet offer an incentive in the form of a rebate to the school as a donation.

I thought it through and started a campaign called "Operation Education" and did that very thing. As students used my service, I kept track of each invoice and then gave the school a 5 percent donation of the total. I received a tax deduction for my donation and was helping the school in return. Finally, since I took her advice and was donating to the school there was an added bonus . . . she ran my ads for free.

There are options to take mobile advertising to a new level. Consider a car wrap. It's a fast-growing trend in marketing and is quickly becoming the preferred form of outdoor mobile advertising. The computer repair industry is a competitive environment, and a vehicle graphic can easily be installed on your car or truck to promote your business twenty-four hours a day!

As a way to communicate with your customers at the lowest cost per impression, a car wrap offers one of the biggest bangs for the buck of any advertising medium. All you need to do is your daily routine and your vehicle does the hard part—the

Old Marketing Still Works

Returning from lunch one day, I noticed that there was an open billboard near my office. I signed a contract, and, within a month, our billboard was up directing traffic via a large arrow and a message that implied "Turn right now to have your cracked screen repaired!" I can attribute about five hundred customers a year to this billboard advertising alone.

I had other friends in other industries who said billboard advertising didn't work for them, so I was skeptical. However, placement and simplicity are key when thinking about running a billboard ad, and I can verify that it works in the right situation.

advertising—for your company. Your vehicle will be in the public eye every day and will hopefully bring in customers as you head to a client's location or head to lunch. Your company-used vehicle is a prime candidate for an advertising wrap—Consider taking it to the next ball game, car race, or rock concert and leave your vehicle near an exit. The exposure will be fantastic! The only downfall to advertising like this is that you're always "on" and you may have a customer approach you when you run to the grocery store or to your child's school concert. Personally I like this approach, but you may not.

If the mobile car-wrap idea is just not your cup of tea, consider a billboard. You can find excellent deals on billboards around most cities; the key is traffic. Do a little research by simply driving around your area and seeing what is available. Start near your office location and you might just find that a $300 investment per month is well worth the payback in new customers.

By now, you understand that you're going to need a website. Yes, your website will have all of the pertinent information about your business, it will have some fantastic graphics, and it will contain all of the necessary components. You will have an online database and checkout system. Now let's talk about these amazing things called the Internet and e-commerce.

It is helpful to have a good mental image of "regular" commerce first. If you understand commerce, then e-commerce is an easy transition.

Merriam-Webster's Collegiate Dictionary gives the definition of commerce:

> *com·merce n [MF, fr. L commercium, fr. com- + merc-, merx merchandise] (1537)*
> *1: social intercourse: interchange of ideas, opinions, or sentiments*
> *2: the exchange or buying and selling of commodities on a large scale involving transportation from place to place.*

So commerce is, quite simply, the exchange of goods and services, usually for money. We see commerce all around us on a daily basis. As consumers, we partake in the action of commerce continuously. When you buy something at a grocery store, you are participating in commerce. In the same way, if you hold a garage sale at your house, you are participating in commerce from a different angle. If you go to work each day for a company that produces a product, that is yet another link in the chain of commerce. When you think about commerce in these different ways, you instinctively recognize several different roles. There are buyers, sellers, and producers.

You can see that at this high level, commerce is a fairly simple concept. Whether it is something as simple as a person mixing and selling lemonade on a street corner or as complex as a contractor delivering a nuclear warhead to the government, all commerce at its simplest level relies on buyers, sellers, and producers.

When you get down to the actual brass tacks of commerce and commercial transactions, things get slightly more complicated because you have to deal with the details. However, these details boil down to a finite number of steps. Let's take a look at a list that highlights the basics. In this case, the activity is the sale of a computer repair to an end-user customer:

1. If you would like to sell something such as a service to a customer, at the very core of the matter is the service itself. You must offer the service on the web. The service may include a product (such as a part that will be installed) and can be anything from a screw set to a hard drive. You may get your products directly from a producer, or you might go through a distributor to get them, but you will produce the service yourself.

2. You must also have a place from which to sell your services. The concept of place can sometimes be very vague. For example, in e-commerce a website is the place. If your customer is in need of a laptop screen repair and places an order on your website for this service, if you fulfill this service then the website is the place where the customer purchased it. For most physical products we tend to think of the place as a store or shop of some sort. But if you think about it a bit more you realize that the place for your sales to occur might primarily be on your website.

3. You need to figure out a way to get people to come to your place. This process is known as marketing. If no one knows that your place exists, you will never sell anything. Locating your place in a busy shopping center is one way to get traffic. Sending out a mail-order catalog is another. There is also advertising, word of mouth, and even the guy in a Statue of Liberty suit who stands by the road waving at passing cars.

4. You need a way to accept orders. At a grocery store this is handled by the checkout line. In a mail-order company, the orders come in by mail or phone and are processed by employees of the company. Ideally your website will check out the customer for you.

5. You also need a way to accept money. If you are at the grocery store, you know that you can use cash, check, or credit cards to pay for food. Business-to-business transactions often use net terms purchase orders.

6. You need a way to deliver the service, often known as fulfillment. At the grocery store, fulfillment is automatic. The customer picks up the item desired, pays for it, and walks out the door. In mail-order businesses the item is packaged and mailed.

7. Sometimes customers do not like what they buy, so you need a way to accept returns. You may or may not charge certain fees for returns, and you may or may not require the customer to get authorization before returning anything. This is up to you, but to obtain a merchant account from your bank, they will require you to have a return policy in place. Additionally, it's just good customer service.

8. Sometimes a product breaks or you make a mistake in its installation, so you need a way to honor warranty claims. Since you're the producer of the service, the warranty claim falls onto you.

9. Many products today are so complicated that they require customer service and technical support departments to help customers use them. Computers are a good example of this sort of product, and many customers have technical questions after a repair is completed. Traditional items (for example, a sack of potatoes from the grocery store) generally require less support than modern electronic items.

In addition, there is often a strong desire to integrate other business functions or practices into the e-commerce offering. An extremely simple example—you might want to be able to show the customer the exact status of an order with an order login link. Nifty!

There are so many examples of good businesses running successful e-commerce campaigns, it's hard not to notice and get excited. Know now that a good website cannot be created overnight and will take time. A careful and well thought out approach will pay off once you can get your website to work for you.

There is a "lure" of e-commerce and it clearly affected me and my way of doing business. The bottom line is that it provides me with lower transaction costs, and I've found a well-implemented website will significantly lower order-taking costs, personnel costs, and customer-service costs. The web is an amazing thing and when you automate some of these functions, you'll see profits rise.

The next lure is that traditionally you will see larger purchases per transaction. You can add suggestions to the bottom of each service you offer, like cases, power

Make Your Website Work

My business takes orders over the phone. I have a straightforward electronics repair company that offers repairs on a multitude of items, and I offer simple mail-in and delivery options to any location in the United States. Initially, I placed ads in magazines, newspapers, and really pushed my customers to call in to speak to a live representative so that we could fulfill a repair order. Mail-order and "catalog-order" sales are standard ways of doing business that have been around for over a century. Sears after all was originally a mail-order company that touted their catalog for decades. About 75 percent of my business's orders move over the web instead of through the telephone. What's the big deal? Does it really matter?

The answer is yes. Even if I moved all 75 percent of my e-commerce business back to phone sales, I would have to hire ten more people. These ten people would need phones, workstations, training, insurance, vacations, and sick time. These ten people would raise the payroll of my small business to a new height. I would need to absorb the costs associated with these ten new employees and that would be damaging to my business. Quite frankly, my e-commerce solution converts more accessories and specials into sales, so I would have to count on my employees to make the proper upsells every time they took an order. With my e-commerce solution, I don't need to worry about that: It's automatic.

Now what if, in the process of selling services over the web, I lost no sales through my traditional phone channel? The fact is that there just happens to be a percentage of people who prefer to buy over the web. Perhaps they give themselves a chance to compare prices, read reviews, or simply just don't like talking on the phone. In my quest to conquer the e-commerce world, I try to build my site to attract buyers and steer customers away from other competitive websites that offer a lesser service. I call this a clear advantage for the business that spends time on its website.

Finally, there is a widely held belief that once a customer starts working with a business, it is much easier to keep that customer than it is to bring in new customers. So if you can build brand loyalty for a website early, it gives you an advantage over other businesses that try to enter the market later. We implemented our website very early, and that presumably gives us an advantage over the competition.

adapters, and headphones if you decide to stock and offer these items. Customers commonly add these items to their order and therefore raise their cart price.

Customers love e-commerce solutions too. Adding a "track your repair" link highly encourages customers to visit the site to see the progress of their service, versus calling in for a status update. One less call means that you can keep working on the important things, such as getting that repair done.

E-commerce also gives customers the ability to shop in their pajamas. I do it. There's no better time for me to go shopping than just before bedtime after a busy day at the office. They can comparison shop, read about you, and order online twenty-four hours per day.

Your website can store a huge amount of information. After a year of being in business, I had twelve hundred services offered on my company's website. After five years we have over five thousand. I don't need a retail store or a humongous catalog to keep all of this information organized—just a well-laid-out website that boasts seamless customer interactions. With automated tools it is possible to interact with a customer in smarter ways at virtually no cost. For example, the customer might get an e-mail when the order is confirmed, when the order is shipped, and after the order arrives to see if they are happy with the service they received. A happy customer is more likely to purchase something else from the company.

It is these sorts of advantages that create the buzz that surrounds e-commerce. There is one final point for e-commerce that needs to be made. E-commerce allows people to create completely new business models that are only conceivable with the Internet, but the caveat is that the website presented on the Internet needs to be found by customers. E-commerce is only as good as its "findability." Remember this: search engine optimization. We will talk about SEO shortly.

However, it is important to point out that the impact of e-commerce only goes so far. It doesn't stop your town from having a mall. The mall has social and entertainment aspects that attract people, and at the mall you can touch the product and make a purchase instantly. E-commerce cannot offer any of these features and retail stores are not going away anytime soon. In fact, you may have a competitor right down the street, in a gorgeous new building. It's OK. There's room for us all; just beat him on the Internet and get your e-commerce game down. You're in control.

Search Engine Optimization

Search engine optimization, otherwise known as SEO, is simply the process of making your website come up when a user searches a particular keyword in a search engine. Basically, it's the search results from a web search.

Why is this important? The search results, unlike the pay-per-click results that we spoke about earlier, are natural search results and don't cost you anything when a customer clicks your link.

Let's take an example: Visit www.google.com, and in the search box, type in "auto repair," then click "Google Search." The page that displays is the search results page. You may see, at the top of the page and down the right hand side of the page, the "pay-per-click" ads that vendors are paying for. Anyone can pay for these ads.

Below the paid ads, you will find the natural search results. You cannot "buy" this placement. You must earn it.

You earn it by offering a complete and comprehensive website that will rise naturally to the top of the listings because your website is the most relevant to the search requested. For example, at the top of my natural results is "About.com's DIY Auto Repair Help." Your results may vary depending on many different factors. However, the point is that About.com's website was listed as the first site for my search query "auto repair" because that site has fantastic SEO.

SEO is an art form. There are many theories about the secret to SEO, but don't let anyone fool you. Google changes the requirements all the time. There is no one secret to being the first result after a search, and in fact two different users might get two different results, even if they search the same thing at the same time. It's part of Google's formula to produce a list that's tailored to your trends and viewing history, not someone else's.

SEO is important. There are basics that must be followed and a bare minimum of SEO techniques to be used if you want to rank at all in the search results. For now, getting your webpage to even show up naturally on the first page is an accomplishment, even if you search your own domain name!

The key is content. In other words, good quality "words" on your website. If you want to have your site come up when a customer searches "auto repair," but you cover your website with the words "car repair," you cannot expect to achieve good results. Instead, you must write keyword-rich content and add it to the pages of your website. This is basic SEO and a small part of your overall SEO game plan.

Reaching Your Market

It's time to implement your marketing plan and begin reaching your market. It's easy to see that social media is more than getting the most fans or "likes." It's truly about building meaningful relationships over time with the right group of people.

This doesn't happen overnight. This is why you need to implement your marketing plan simultaneously while building your online trust and community. It will take time, but with time you can build authentic relationships with your online and live followers. Drive real sales and capture measurable business value from all of your hard work.

I've said it before and I'll say it again. The more I type, the more sales I make.

This belief comes from dealing directly with customers on a daily basis and understanding them. I want to know what drives them and what moves them into action to use my services. I personally tend not to limit my geographical audience. I want to reach everyone. However, in the beginning this is typically not plausible, so you should focus on a region, like your own city, to start.

You'll need business cards, and when you're ready to reach new clients that will be an extremely important part of your plan. The phone number on your business card should ring your location during your normal operating hours. There are two reasons for this: The first is because you are a service company, and no single statement communicates a stronger commitment to service than answering the phone. Second, when you drop off a business card to a receptionist and ask him or her to "please give it to the IT manager or other person in charge of computer maintenance," it's important to answer when you get a callback. Your business card will be the link to your business and effectively the "roadmap" a customer will follow to reach you. That's reaching your market.

This strategy is ancient, tested, and reliable. The only way it can fail is if you don't walk in enough doors. Do you have the discipline to walk into fifty new businesses every day when business is slow? If you do this faithfully, you will have called on 250 businesses at the end of a week, 1,000 in a month, and your business will easily increase.

Let's take this example a step farther, and since we're really talking about e-commerce, we need to make sure that each visit leads not only to your telephone, but also to your website. All those customers whom you approach will most likely visit your website first before calling you. List your website prominently below or even above the telephone number on your business card. Since your website is your silent salesperson, the link between your visit and a sale might just be your site. Think about the number of people who won't walk into a business and ask for service. Having your website answer the common questions for those shy or introverted customers will help you reach them, even though you may never be able to meet them face to face or speak to them on the phone. Catering to personality types is a skill that the best salespeople have, and not discriminating against a certain type of customer is the winning answer.

Getting Listed in Directories

Getting your website listed in directories is important as a source of traffic to your site but also because they help the search engines understand which market or topic your site pertains to. Even more importantly, it's a free service. This can make your site extremely relevant within search results, therefore offering your site higher listings in the search engines. Directories are controlled by real people who look at the content of websites that are submitted and place them in the relevant categories to assure accuracy.

Additionally, search engines like Google and Yahoo reach into directory listings, so this is a good way of getting your site indexed initially on the Internet.

Yahoo is the largest and best-known directory, with experts who review sites before indexing them.

Dmoz.org is a directory that is important to your business because it is used by Google for the Google directory pages and also by many other directory sites.

To get listed in a directory, simply visit the directory site and submit your website's information. Don't be surprised if your website doesn't show up immediately. Remember that these sites are run by employees and volunteers who sift through thousands of requests daily. Be patient, and don't submit more than once.

Link Exchange

Link exchange, or reciprocal links, is important for your website to be "visible" on the Internet. The Internet is based on links, and if you find a great site that you love, you should provide a link to it. Now you don't want to go crazy here. Linking to other sites will help them become more visible and "findable" on the Internet and is considered a courtesy to your visitors.

Ask yourself why visitors are on your website. Give them what they want and what they are looking for. In addition, you can help your visitors by offering them a link to a related website. Links to related sites show that you care about them. You should always build your website with your visitor in mind.

Be logical, though—don't send your visitors to a competitor unless you'd prefer to help that competitor make a few sales. The link should be to a site that offers information or advice on a topic that is related to computer repair. For example, if you're servicing Dell laptops, you might have a link to Dell's website.

The idea, however, is to get Dell to post a link back to your website. That might prove to be difficult, as Dell doesn't necessarily care about your small business, nor do they believe that you can help them as much as they can help you.

So the key is to find like-minded sites—other small businesses, rumor sites, blogs, and informational sites that you might be able to link to. Once you do, send the owner of the site an e-mail and ask for a link back.

Once you have a few links, it will be called a link directory. A good link directory is a valuable resource for your visitors and it improves the content of your website. If your website contains many related links for a specific topic, chances are that your website will be considered an authority on that topic by customers and search engines.

Well-designed link pages with useful and related links help you to make your website more attractive to visitors. Websites that are useful and attractive for web surfers get high search-engine rankings because they're considered authorities and worth linking to.

Focus on your website visitors. Search engines try to find websites that are useful for website visitors. If the linking structure of your website indicates that it is a useful site, your site will get great search engine rankings as well as targeted traffic from your link partners.

Building an E-Mail List

Here's an easy one. E-mail "blasts" are nothing new, and there are services that you can use to help you with these, but also look at your e-commerce provider as well. Many of them will offer e-mail newsletter services as part of a package deal.

What can you do with an e-mail list? The idea behind the e-mail list is that you've got a specific list of customers who are interested in what you have to offer—specifically meaning that they want to hear from you. I've always had a "sign up for our newsletter here" widget on my website that takes a customer e-mail address and stores it in a list for future use. The best part about this list is that it consists of quality e-mail addresses, not just random addresses that have no meaning to you or your business.

E-mail marketing is not dead, contrary to some professionals. Trust me on this. If it were, then why does almost every site you visit, when you sign up for an account, ask you for your e-mail address when the account is created? It's because an e-mail address is unique to you and a direct way to send you promotions and other pertinent information that you can choose to read or delete.

The benefit of a quality e-mail list is that when you send correspondence to your customers via e-mail it can be personal. E-mail is a personal thing. You can keep it casual and friendly, and it's a great way to build trust with your subscribers.

Additionally, e-mail is direct. There's no middleman or pop-up window to work around. You send an e-mail directly to the customer who is interested in what you have to say!

Finally, it's a private thing. People can sit down and read e-mail on their own time, reply if they'd like, ask questions, and feel the open communication between you and them. It's not like replying on a blog or forum where everyone can see and read comments. E-mail is intended only for its recipient.

The best way to build your e-mail list is to have a signup form on the home page of your website. It needs to be obvious and inviting. When customers enter their e-mail addresses, they "opt-in" to receive communication from you, so it's an open invitation to connect.

When you do connect, you can send offers, specials, or simply send a weekly newsletter about how business is going, how you're improving, or other positive points that you want to convey.

Tap into the power of the e-mail list and you just might become a newsletter fanatic.

Online Auctions

There's another way to make sales, and that's to run auctions on eBay. I know, you're a computer repair shop, right? Well, run an auction for a computer repair and you will sell it.

Using eBay can be a very powerful tool, and in fact for a new business it's a classic way to start selling immediately. It's relatively easy, and if you've never sold on eBay before, there are tutorials that walk you through each step of the process. All you'll need is your computer, an Internet connection, and your repair services. The auction process will handle the rest.

Another powerful aspect of eBay is that the SEO value is tremendous. eBay auctions immediately show up on the first page of Google searches most of the time, and being on the first page of Google is the key to natural sales. eBay is a powerful website, and Google rewards eBay by providing relevant auctions in top spots. Give it a try: Perform a Google search for a product that you'd normally buy online, and I bet there will be an eBay auction as part of the search results. If that auction leads to a sale for you, you can thank me later.

Finally, eBay is exciting. It's exciting to watch bidders ramp up your price, and it's exciting to see a customer complete an auction. Typically you'll get an e-mail with a "Your Item Sold" subject line, and when that happens, you're excited to find out that you just sold a product or a service and never had to pick up the phone!

E-Commerce Worksheet

Go through this list to make sure you're on the right e-commerce path. There will be other necessary pieces of e-commerce trade that you may find along the way and you should increase your reach as you prefer.

- ☐ Launch a website.
- ☐ Make it easy for your customers to find services on your website.
- ☐ Market your website.
- ☐ Add a shopping-cart component to your website.
- ☐ Accept credit cards on your website.
- ☐ Be prepared to ship orders back to customers.
- ☐ Have a clear return policy on your website.
- ☐ Offer warranties on your services and technical support.
- ☐ Learn and master SEO techniques.
- ☐ Network yourself and your website.
- ☐ Get listed on Internet directories.
- ☐ Participate in link exchanges with other sites.
- ☐ Build an e-mail list and write a newsletter.
- ☐ Offer a few products and services on eBay.

11 | Business Endgame

Do you stick with it? Do you grow it? Do you sell it? In my mind, those are the three obvious options. You have to decide what's best for you and your business. There are many schools of thought that drive this type of decision making for business owners and operators. Many of your trusted advisors will have their personal opinions, and they will share them. Again, you have to decide what's best for you and your business.

From my personal experiences, I have learned that I must weigh my options and take the time to consider the consequences of each choice. Not only is my business my livelihood, and that of my family, but I have to consider my employees as well. No two businesses are alike and therefore no two situations can be handled the same. Making rash decisions has never served me well. I have to think about tomorrow and long term. So often unforeseen problems, expenses, and profits creep out of nowhere. Having taken the time to anticipate as many of these unknown factors as possible has served me, and my business, well.

Take it from me. Starting and running your own business is tough but also very rewarding. The three questions above will be a part of your daily life for as long as you own your own business, just like checking your bank accounts and "numbers." Don't allow yourself to get burned out. Don't allow yourself to fall into a negative frame of mind when managing people and money. Take each day one step at a time. Watch the competition, research your options, rationally problem-solve through the trials, and enjoy the success. You will find that the feelings of pride and accomplishment were worth all of the blood, sweat, and tears.

I wish you the very best!

Status Quo: Is It for You?

There will be a time when you can sit back and say that you've gotten things under control. This is a great feeling, but as an entrepreneur you're wired with success in mind and growth may be inevitable. There's nothing wrong with a consistent business. When you find that balance, the fact of the matter is that once your initial growth trend stops—which may take years—you'll find that leveling off and reaching consistent sales numbers each month is when you'll really start to make some profits. It's an interesting dynamic that I didn't understand until I saw it within my own company.

Your goal in the business world and as an owner/operator may be that you'll work the business, hopefully with the help of your future employees, until you are ready to retire. This is a healthy way of thinking as most of us will work until retirement age, and "striking gold" or "getting rich quick" mentalities need to be left to those lucky individuals who have those experiences.

Getting your business to show a stable profit-and-loss statement is plenty of work for any new owner. In fact, your P&L will be your guide through the years and is an excellent snapshot of the health of the business each month.

Growing Your Business to New Heights

At first glance the term "growing" translates to "more sales," which means "more money." Unfortunately it also means "more overhead." When you grow you might need more space (rent), more employees (payroll), and more tools (capital equipment). You need to decide whether to push forward and grow or keep your business in your comfort zone.

Just as growing your business is costly and stressful, it has its good points. A growing business means job security. When you land a large client or your marketing plan really kicks in and starts bringing in more customers each month, you find yourself with a good problem to have. I consider too much business a problem, but it's a good problem. Remember that you're in the service business and your reputation is your most valuable asset. Since you're the best in the business, more customers will come your way. In fact, at some point you will reap the benefit and enjoy a word-of-mouth increase in customers.

The key to growing is being able to maintain your reputation, turnaround time, and business model while adding expense and sales. It sounds like an easy task but trust me it can quickly turn from a "good problem" to "business killer."

Is Growth the Key?

Have you ever heard the phrase "Growing too fast can put you out of business"?

In my mind, I thought that growth was the key to success. It is in a way, and most business owners embrace growth and look forward to the challenge of beating sales goals, adding inventory, and adding employees.

The real issue with growth is that it is expensive. In most cases, when you grow it means that you need to spend more money. When you spend more money to grow, the expense typically comes before you reap the rewards. So month after month, I grew my business. Year after year, I grew my business. I was always thrilled that I was beating my previous month's sales numbers and making new records. What I was missing out on was consistent sales numbers. My growth was expensive, and even though I was increasing my top line, my bottom line was not increasing as I had hoped.

Find your sweet spot. Make a determination about how big you want to get, get there, and steady yourself. As your business slows from a growth mode to more of a consistent monthly sales number, you'll find that profits will compound quickly and you will start to enjoy the trend.

It's basically all about managing your cash flow. Many times entrepreneurs get overly engaged in the joy of growth and lose sight of the need to manage cash on a daily basis. This might sound simple, but it can be a major issue if not handled properly. Business owners have to understand that we may not be able to afford all the available growth. The amount of cash available for investment can limit growth, especially in today's economy, when many small businesses can't get loans or credit lines. I can't help but stress the importance of cautiously managing your checkbooks, credit cards, and online accounts.

So if you're on a growth path and it's where you want to stay, remember that you need to know when to say no. Once established, your business will have countless opportunities, and the challenge is to choose the opportunities that work well for you. Some of this will be trial and error, but if you approach each new project from a logical perspective, you will see the shortfalls and make an educated decision. The point is that you don't want to lose your focus and dilute your efforts by taking on projects or clients that don't work for you.

To continue your growth path, you're going to need to effectively delegate. You must grow as well. You can only do so much in a single day, and growing your business will mean hiring people to assist you with your expanding reach. The problem is that you're the creator of the business and it's hard to let go of some duties. It's like sending your child to school for the first time. You want to be there and make sure that everything goes well, but you have to understand that it's better for the child to get an education and learn from another adult. You'll have to let go.

Additionally, you'll need to transition from the "owner" to a "leader." This is a tough thing to do. You might be perfectly suited to run your own business, but to keep it healthy and running with multiple employees, you will need to lead. In fact, I call it "cheerleading" because that it what it is at times. Keeping your employees motivated and working in the company's best interest is a delicate balance. You will need to discipline, praise, reward, and congratulate your employees when they produce for you. But don't expect praise in return—it's lonely at the top.

So hire smart. Hiring mistakes are costly and time consuming. Training your employees will cost money too. So make sure that you don't waste too much time on a bad egg. If you see a problem, nip it in the bud. I found that instead of looking for fully qualified people for specific positions, I preferred to hire like-minded people and then train them "my way." This was a lot of work, but it proved to work well for me because their expectations were clearly laid out and I started our business relationship by working closely together.

This in turn creates a highly efficient team and "family." I like to address my group of employees as a "team" because that is really what we all are. The struggle with this concept is when a member of the team stands out as the weak link and often, as the business grows, there is a team member who cannot grow with it. It's about creating clear expectations and job descriptions for your employees so they have the opportunity to excel.

The bottom line is that growing a business is an evolutionary process. It can be messy and it most certainly is changeable—but it's about learning and taking risks. Just what the entrepreneur ordered!

When It's Time to Sell

There are some common questions asked by owners who are considering selling their business. One of the initial concerns is about timing the sale with an upswing in the business-sales market—it just makes sense to try to sell your business when the market is swelling. Of course you will be considering all aspects of your business when it comes time to sell, but what will be most important (other than market conditions) will be the state of the business and what you will want out of the deal.

You will need to carefully consider the current state of your business. There's something to be said for a business with a long track record of increasing sales and profits. Conversely, if you think that you can build a business and "flip" it within the first year, don't be surprised to find that there aren't buyers lining up at your doorstep ready to write big checks. Even if you're showing phenomenal profits, a one-year history is just too risky for most people to invest in.

The current condition of your individual business is a significant factor in timing its sale. Businesses that show a strong track record of steady or increasing sales and profitability will always sell faster and for a better price than those that are in a decline. If your business is up or steady, it is a good time to sell. No matter the external economic factors surrounding your company, if your business is up, the demand for it and the sales price will follow. Furthermore, there's a perception in the investor's world that a business that's doing $10 million per year in sales is a desirable entity. It's just a benchmark number. Of course profits need to be there as well as a steady and consistent flow of good business. If you have a business that's doing $10 million per year, you can expect a different kind of buyer, a serious buyer, and you will enjoy a bidding war to take you over.

The most important factor in selling your business will be your personal goals during the process and beyond. Whatever the reasons for the sale of the business (retirement, distress, and health being the most common), if it is the right time for the owners, it is usually the best time to sell. By waiting or delaying the sale as a result of speculation about current market conditions, owners may be putting themselves in a bad position. There are many sad stories of owners who have underestimated the time to properly market, sell, and transfer a business. They waited too long to begin the process and found themselves in a highly compromising situation as they went to sell their company. The amount of time an owner has to sell a company will directly affect the way it is marketed and priced. The more time you have, the better. In a worst-case scenario, time can destroy the chances of selling your business for a fair price when you are faced with a drop-dead date by which the business must be sold. There are circumstances that necessitate a "fire sale," but you can't expect good results under these conditions.

Just remember that as with most things in life, timing is everything. If you start a business with the intention of selling it as a top priority, take your time. Weigh the options, and grow the business's value. Having a business that is "sell-worthy" is a feat in itself and you should be commended for it. While being commended is a nice thing, being financially rewarded is another. Fine-tune it and set it out to market. Then retire and buy that island you've been dreaming about. I'll pack my bathing suit.

Concluding Thoughts

The people who know me best will often hear me say, "That's it!" And it's true—this really is it. Think about the gem you are holding in your hands. Not only do you have an outline for just about every step of launching your home-based computer repair business, but you also have access to many documents, references, and websites to help you personalize every decision, right here at your fingertips. In addition, you've got many of my personal tips, tricks, and pieces of advice. Yes, I really did share a few of my secrets and a few of my failures because I wanted you to see the reality behind the author. I am a real man, a real business owner. I have been where you are. I have lived in the trenches of the first months of opening my own business. Hopefully sharing many of my trials and successes will help you to avoid some pitfalls and find your own personal accomplishments. That's the reason I wrote this book. Just as I want to treat my customers the way I would want to be treated, I wanted to write a book that would help the everyday Joes, like myself, find their own niche in the world of entrepreneurship.

Yes, you read that correctly. "Everyday Joes." You, me, any one of my employees can start his or her own business. That is not to say that starting your own business is for the faint of heart. It requires common sense, hard work, and passion. It doesn't require that a person enter the area of business ownership already rich. The only things one must be rich in to do this job are character and work ethic.

Work ethic. A trait found in some that drives their desire and ability to be the very best. I've said it once and I'll say it again: Starting your own business isn't easy. If I weren't driven by my desire to work for myself in an industry I am passionate about, while providing the best possible service to the public, I couldn't be the owner of a successful business. This is not a nine-to-five job. Because I work for myself, it doesn't mean I go into the office whenever I please, take long vacations multiple times a year, and make a salary that is more than my fair share based on the work I do. I have to be wise and rational in my decision making. That takes ethics.

One last word to the wise . . . the Internet is an amazing tool. Never forget that. Use it to your advantage. Not only can you learn from the Internet by using it for research, you can also use the web to network, market, and complete day-to-day tasks that are essential to running your own business. You surfed the web for information to build your business plan. You hopped online to find the number of a lawyer or graphic designer or maintenance person. It's great that you have all of that settled, but that doesn't mean the days of using the Internet to search out solutions to your everyday questions and problems are over. No such luck, my friend. The "net" will be the first place you turn when in need of anything. From tools and parts to employees and insurance, the Internet will become your new best friend.

I begin the day using the Internet to handle my online banking, and I end the day using the Internet to keep my thumb on all possible sales trends within the business that day. My business website is the heart and face of my company. It's what allowed for those sales that I tracked all day. Without the Internet, and therefore my website, my business likely wouldn't be possible. I would have to rely solely on marketing to find my success. Can you even imagine what marketing would look like without the web? The cost? The effort? I cringe at the thought.

What has online marketing brought me that is so vitally important, you might ask? The networking! Without the Internet to help facilitate word of mouth, where would businesses be? Without the Internet to link one business to another, how would customers search out and locate services they need? How would I be able to keep my eye on the competition and stay one step ahead? Sounds dramatic I know, but I think I got your attention and drove my point home. Don't ever underestimate the power of the Internet when coupled with your ethics, drive, and passion.

Appendix

As you check out some of these resources, you may find help just around the corner from many companies and individuals alike. Please always fully investigate each using your own judgment, while always adhering to state and federal government laws as they apply to your business. There are many rules and regulations that need to be followed, and certainly not every relevant resource will be listed in this appendix, but maybe a few of these will be valuable to you.

This is not a complete list. Every day, new publications are produced that should be read and understood. Remember to count on the team of professionals that you will surround yourself with as you gain experience and knowledge.

I'll always be here for you, and I wish you good luck and huge success.

Business Resources

Entrepreneur
"10 Tips for the First-Time Business
    Owner."
entrepreneur.com/article/203254

Google Webmaster Tools
Free and helpful advice to rank on
    Google.
google.com/webmaster/tools

IRS
"Tax Information for Businesses"
irs.gov/Businesses

Qualdev
E-commerce solution website.
qualdev.com

Small Business Administration
For all of your small business questions
    and advice.
sba.gov

Volusion
E-commerce solution website.
volusion.com

Yahoo! Small Business
Website dedicated to helping get small
    businesses online.
smallbusiness.yahoo.com

Advertising Sources

@List
Directory for listing your website.
alist.org

Bizweb
Directory for listing your website.
bizweb.com

DMOZ
Directory for listing your website.
dmoz.org

Facebook Ads
For pay-per-click advertising on
    Facebook.
facebook.com/Ads

Fathom SEO
Professional SEO Marketing Company.
fathomdelivers.com

Google Adwords
For pay-per-click advertising on Google.
adwords.google.com

Groupon
Advertising resource with no up-front
    costs to the business.
groupon.com

Transworld News
Press-release service that offers annual
    subscriptions.
transworldnews.com

Trade Shows

CES
An enormous trade show held in Las
    Vegas each January all about con-
    sumer electronics.
cesweb.org

CTIA
Wireless communications tradeshow.
ctia.org

Macworld
A long-running trade show with celebrity speakers.
macworldiworld.com

Topline
A large directory of trade shows held throughout the year.
topline.tv/tradeshow.cfm

Educational Resources

Apple Certification
Become a Macintosh Technician.
training.apple.com/certification

CompTIA
Get IT certified.
certification.comptia.org

CTS
Computer Training Schools.
computertrainingschools.com

Prometric Testing Centers
Located around the country for final technician exams.
prometric.com

Social-Networking Sites

Facebook
facebook.com

LinkedIn
linkedin.com

Twitter
twitter.com

Pinterest
pinterest.com

Other Websites You Might Find Helpful

GoDaddy
Domain name registration.
godaddy.com

PayPal
Another bank service that is being widely adopted.
paypal.com

PaySimple
Merchant account provider for Visa, Mastercard, and American Express.
paysimple.com/merchant_account
.html

Index

objectives, 63
plan for, 64–65
publicity, 154–58
social-media, 142–45
Super Bowl ads, 154
traditional, 145–47
websites in, 139
market segmentation, 65–66
mats, electrostatic discharge, 44
Microsoft Excel, 54
Microsoft Office, 54
Microsoft PowerPoint, 54
Microsoft Word, 54
mindset, 6–7
mission, 62
mobile advertising, 158–60

N
"named" telephone numbers, 51
naming your business, 26–27, 29–30
navigation, website, 73–74, 77
networking, 142
newspaper advertising, 146
niche, finding, 11–16
"no," knowing when to say, 174

O
objectives, 62–63
office space. *See* workspace
office supplies, 22
ongoing expenses, 108
online auctions, 170–71
operating expenses, 108
operating hours, 10–11, 40
operations (business plan), 66–67
organization, 41, 58, 59

P
paperless system, 129–30
partnerships, 24, 25, 26
patience, 137
paycheck, first, 123
Pay-Per-Click, 150

PCs niche, 13–14
personal credit, 118
personnel plan, 67
phone service, 22–23, 50–53
pitch letters, 155, 157–58
power outlets, 44
Presence (VoIP feature), 52
press releases, 155, 156–57
prestige prices, 99
pricing, 37, 97–100
printers, 21
privacy statement, 78–81
private labeling, 102
products
    bundled, 104
    in business plan, 64
    buying low, 122
    cross-selling, 103–5
    refurbished, 105–6
profit-and-loss statement (P&L), 108, 110–12,
    117–18
profit margin, 101
property insurance, 86–87
psychological prices, 99
publicity, 154–58
purchase orders, 94–95
pushiness, 105

Q
quality control, 37–38, 102
quotes, 92–94

R
reach, expanding, 139–42
reaching your market, 167–68
receipts, 38–39, 128
receiving space, 44, 46
reciprocal links, 168–69
record-keeping, 129–30
refurbished products, 105–6
reliability, 3, 33
repeat business, 33–34
retail shopping center buildings, 49
return materials authorization (RMA) rate, 38